[2011]

OAK ISLAND Mystery FINALLY SOLVED !!!

Oak Island, Nova Scotia

the **OAK ISLAND MYSTERY**

For 200 years men & women have lost everything, even their lives & families, to the mystery of this island.
It keeps its secrets to this day.

Dr. G. Chopra / Simran

Table of Contents

Preface	4
Introduction	8
The Good NEWS	14
Packing Up… The journey begins	16
Packing Up… The journey begins	16
The Research	24
The Discovery of the Oak Island Money Pit	25
The New Journey – A new discovery	31
The Family Ventures out	44
Missing - Mr Smith	54
The Team proceeds…	74
The Truth is reveled…	82
The CODE……	85
The Conspiracy…	98
The Code finally revealed….	103
The 1st leg….	110
Link to the Treasure…	117
Bank of England Connection…	125
Watch out Brits…	128
Research in Rome getting deep…	135

The final countdown… A shocker…	147
Anti Christ Connection 666 or 616	155
Royalty at the doorstep…	161

Preface

Oak Island is a 140-acre (57 ha) island in Lunenburg County on the south shore of Nova Scotia, Canada. The tree-covered island is one of about 360 small islands in Mahone Bay and rises to a maximum of 35 feet (11 m) above sea level. Located 200 metres from shore and connected to the mainland by a modern causeway, the island is privately owned, and advance permission is required for any visitation.

Oak Island is noted as the location of the so-called Money Pit and the site of over 200 years of treasure hunting. Repeated excavations have reported layers of apparently man-made artifacts as deep as 31 meters, but ended in collapsed excavations and flooding. Critics argue that there is no treasure and that the pit is a natural phenomenon, likely a sinkhole.

The story goes something like this. Oak Island is located off the coast of Nova Scotia, Canada. One day in 1795 a teenager named Daniel McGinnis made his way to the island to explore it. He happened upon an oak tree (one of many on the island) which caught his eye because hanging from one outstretched limb was an old pulley. The type used to raise and lower heavy items. It was situated directly over a large circular depression in the ground. Realizing what this might be he returned the next day with two friends, Anthony Vaughan and John Smith. They began digging with picks and shovels. It was clear by the marks on the side of the hole that it had been dug my men and then refilled. . At the 2 foot mark they hit a layer of flagstones. They removed them and continued digging. At the 10 foot level they hit wood. Visions of pirate treasure danced in their heads. There were many stories circulating during that time of treasure belonging to the infamous pirate Captain Kidd being buried on some island. The wood turned out to be oak logs. Removing the logs revealed a two foot gap and then more dirt. As they continued digging they found another layer of logs at 20 feet and again at 30 feet. At this point they realized they needed more help and more equipment so they left the island with the idea of returning to finish what they started.

It would be 9 years before they returned. This time they were accompanied by Simeon Lynds, a businessman. He provided the labor force and financial backing to continue the dig. They found the site as they had left it. They began digging. At 40 feet they found a layer of charcoal. At 50 feet they found a layer of putty. At 60 feet, a layer of coconut fiber. At the 90 foot mark they discovered a stone tablet inscribed with symbols. These symbols were later translated to say "40 feet below, two million pounds lie buried."

A few feet below the tablet the tunnel began to flood. Unable to bail the water from the tunnel faster than it filled the group gave up.

Theories

There are many theories as to what lies at the bottom of the pit and there are numerous websites dedicated to proving each theory. Some of the more popular ones are:

Captain Kidd's treasure – By far the most popular theory but as more information is gathered, this is quickly becoming less likely.

Combined booty of several pirates – An interesting theory presented by a fellow named Samuel Goodman. He believes there are seven maps that when put together reveal the exact location of the treasure. He says he's linked the five maps he knows of together but does not have the final two.

The lost treasure of the Knights Templar – recent findings on the island point to symbols and such used by Freemasons including a giant cross.

Hidden documents belonging to Francis Bacon - You may already be familiar with the idea that William Shakespeare didn't have the education and ability to write the works that are attributed to him. Some suggest that they were actually written by Bacon and the proof for this lies at the bottom of the Money Pit.

Other theories that have less information to support them include

Inca Treasure

French crown jewels

Aliens

My research has been extensively related to world history, historical events, pirate connections and have put all of this in a format which would be fun reading as well as informative for all ages.

Regards

Introduction

The Oak Island Money Pit is the site of the world's longest running hunt for lost treasure. For hundreds of years, treasure hunters have ventured to Nova Scotia and tried to recover the treasure which is protected by a series of ingenious traps. Strange man made artifacts have been recovered from the pit over the years, but to this day, the treasure still remains buried. Pirates, the Knights Templar or Francis Bacon – no one is sure exactly who created this mysterious Money Pit or why. There has been wide-ranging speculation as to who originally dug the pit and what it might contain. Oak platforms were discovered every 10 feet. There were pick scrapes on the walls on the money pit and the dirt was noticeably loose and not as hard packed. The flood tunnel at 90 feet has been identified and known to be lined with flat stones. Some have speculated that the Oak Island pit was dug to hold treasure much more exotic than gold or silver. In his 1953 book, The Oak Island Enigma: A History and Inquiry Into the Origin of the Money Pit, Penn Leary claimed that English philosopher Francis Bacon used the pit to hide documents proving him to be the author of William Shakespeare's plays. In the image above we see the money pit as it appears today. A much more in depth article on the **Oak Island money pit** is available **here**.

It was summer of 2010 Simi 11 years old a smart kid in school helped around the house whenever she could. In one of her chores, she picked up the mail and set it on the table where dad sorts it out and had his evening coffee.

"PAPA here is your mail... let me know if you need help in sorting it out..", she said as she placed the stack of mail on the table....

"Thanks Beta..." he said as he grabbed his cup of coffee. He picked up the stack in one hand his cup of coffee in the other and sat in his easy chair. As he switched on the TV he called his daughter, "Simi... do you want to come over and help me sort this mail".

"Sure papa... "She replied always happy to help papa ....

"Bills, junk, bills, bills.. Junk...", he said as he sorted the mail out and handed the junk mail to Simi...

Normally what Simi did was she would go through the junk mail and see if there are any "cool' things... as she was sorting out she looked at papa with one letter in her hand and said "Papa is this really junk mail ?, looks like an invitation to me looks like you just won something... "

As Singh took the letter from Simran's hand he thought it was just another scam letter – he looked at Simi and read the letter aloud...

"Hello Mr. Singh,

We invite you to a weekend at "Oak Island" and we promise you that this would be the best weekend of your life...

We ask that you solve this problem and send in your answer. Once we select your answer you will get a ticket to "Oak Island" and along with other winners you will have a wonderful weekend.

Question :

"Every deck of cards has four kings.

Every picture of the KING has two faces...

Place the four kings in a way that once you are done only ONE FACE of each king should be visible....

Take a picture and email the picture to

sam@queenofbargains2000.com"

Thanks

Peter.

Mr. Singh looked at Simi and said.... "You want to solve this ?"

'Sure papa, but on one condition, if I solve this and we are selected you are not going to say NO… We all will go and have a good time", she said firmly. Mr Singh agreed, "Ok Simi, no problem…". And hands her the letter - He continues sorting the rest of the mail and throws away the junk, calls out to his wife, " honey the bills are on the table.. when ever you get a chance pl. take care of them"

He stretches and flops back in his easy chair watching TV –

Meanwhile Simi all excited about the potential trip is busy trying to solve the puzzle and look for hints on the internet… she gets some clues and about an hour later she comes running back to the living room…"PAPA PAPA PAPA, guess what ?", all excitedly she says… Mr Singh was asleep in his chair.. but is startled by Simi's sudden burst of excitement… "What's the matter ?"

"I did it .. I did it.. I solved the problem… ", she said handing him the sheet of paper… "Great let me look at it " he said taking the paper from her.. "looks good to me…" he said handing her the paper…

"WHAT ?, aren't you going to send it in ?".. she asked.

"You really want me to ?".. Mr. Singh asked…

"Yes… you never know… !!".. She said shrugging her shoulders…

"OK OK .. hand me that return envelope, I will do it right now…" he said as he pointed over to the stack of envelopes…

He placed the paper in the envelope, filled out their details and said," here you go.. you never know.. next month we could be in OAK ISLAND…"

Simi was all excited she ran to her mother to tell her the news. Mom heard her story and could see the excitement in her daughter's eyes…, "don't worry Simi, even if we don't get a positive response I will have your papa take us there anyways for doing a great job in solving this difficult puzzle…"…

"Thank you mummy, you are the best mummy in the whole wide world… " so no matter what happens we are going to Oak Island… who… hoooooo…" she said as she ran to her room to work on her home work… She pulled out her little diary and wrote… "Simi and family going to Oak Island"…. She then got on the internet and wanted to see what all there was on OAK island that they could see when they got there…. She started making a list of places to visit and things to do….and thought to herself.. I will keep this a secret until we get there and surprise mom and her dad.

Mr Singh was running a consulting business … He helps businesses globally outsource their work and save money. He has been doing this for

over 15 years and his business is pretty much running on cruise control..
"Pinky" as Mr. Singh calls his wife.. is in the medical profession – which keeps her busy… They have a 5 year old son too "JOT" who is the naughty kid in the house. He is full of questions and is a whiz kid himself… reads books and plays with his friends.

Simi is the thread that ties the family together. She is always willing to help and take care of things at school for her friends… She excels in school and is always willing to help her friends with their work... Her friends and teachers love her, they all wished there were more kids like her in school….
This is basically what the Singh family looks like…

The Good NEWS

A s days went along Mr. Singh was busy with his work, Pinky was busy at the hospital, Jot was busy with his antics, but Simi was busy making a list of things to do when they get to OAK ISLAND….

Three weeks later, "Simi… could you go get the mail…" – Mr. Singh called Simi… "Sure papa… " she bolted out and was back with a stack of mail…. As she asked her papa everyday – when she handed him the mail – "don't forget to look for our trip….."

SIMI – DEC 5th

Papa gave Simi a big pile of what he thought was all junk mail, as usual, and Simi started to sort it all out, as usual.

All of a sudden Simi jumped out of her seat and started to jump around with an envelope in her hand. Papa, mama and Jot stared at Simi like she was CRAZY! 'What happened dear?' said mama in a very soft and soothing way. Simi said in a very energetic and exciting way, 'WE'RE GOING TO OAK ISLAND!!!!!!!!!!!!!!!!' When everyone heard the last words Simi said, EVERYONE started to jump around!

When everyone FINALY calmed down, Simi read the letter out loud.............

Dear Mr. Singh,

Your answer was far the most inventive and creative one of all. You and your family have won four tickets to travel to OAK ISLAND for 10 days! The best part is the trip to and back and anywhere you go on OAK ISLAND is totally FREE!!!!!

If you have any questions about the trip you can contact us at our phone number:(519)-632-1897 or you can contact us at www.OAK ISLAND ADVENTURE TRIP. ca.

Sincerely,

The OAK ISLAND staff

Packing Up… The journey begins

"I'm not sure…"said papa uneasily.

"Don't forget the deal that we made, remember papa? Simi said eagerly.

"You're right Simi, we did make a deal, ok okay   lets start packing!' papa said, now excited.

Simi then dashed upstairs, like a lightning bolt, to start packing. Once in her room, Simi pulled out her suitcase from under her bed. It was already half full because she had a feeling that they were going to go. In the suitcase she had put, 5 pairs of skirts, 5 shorts, 35 t-shirts, 35 hair bands that match her clothes, 3 of her favorite pairs of sunglasses, a book, her diary to record all the things that they did, a map of the whole island, another map of all the tourist areas and amusement parks and arcades, and, a list where she wanted to go.

Daddy Dec 7th

"Lalalalaaaaaa".. comes in singing JOT – "can you help me pack ?" asking Simi – "sure, as soon as I am done with mine"… replied Simi…

Both had their bags packed and ready to go… Mom and dad loved the fact that the whole family is going… Mr. Singh called his manager SAM –

explained to him all of the work that needed finished in the next week – and also informed him that he will be traveling with his portable internet so at least once a day he will check his emails and respond…

Mom, Dad, Simi and Jot drove down to the airport – with their bag and baggage – got on the airplane and flew to - Oak Island a 140 acres (57 ha) island in Lunenberg County on the south shore of Nova Scotia, Canada…. The tree-covered island is one of about 360 small islands in Mahone Bay and rises to a maximum of 35 feet (11 m) above sea level. They flew to Nova Scotia – and a car picked them up to take them to the island.

"Hi – I am Mike, this is SAM and Anita – They will be your guides and take you to your residence" … The family all excited – followed them to log cabins to stay in with 4 beds, a small kitchen to cook, and a small bathroom… a sign on the door said "Beware of monkeys"… The family smiled and walked in…

Simi couldn't wait to explore, dad was tired and wanted to rest, mom was setting up the clothes and kitchen… and Jot the youngest brat in the family was busy calling out to monkeys…

Every member was busy… in the evening the kids and mom and dad got together for dinner that Anita brought in. "Tomorrow, you are going to explore this 140 acres and have fun…"

The family got together and held hands prayed before they had their meals, once they were done eating mom went back to the kitchen, dad fired up his laptop and Simran was busy making notes in her diary… while they were all busy JOT walks in with a necklace around his neck….

"What are you wearing ? Where did you get it from ? … mummy… look Jot is wearing one of your necklaces…" Simi called out to her mom…

Mom walks towards him – "No I didn't., my friend gave it to me…" Jot replied… dad was listening to all of this and said "your who??? You have a friend on this island ..? Already!!! That was fast …. "

"Yeah his name is Mangu… he was up on the tree right outside this window – I am not kidding … he smiled at me and I threw an apple at him… I was just playing and in return he threw back this necklace, I watched him eat the apple and I put this necklace in my pocket and came back…" Jot explained…

Dad put his laptop aside and asked Jot to come over – he looked at the necklace – it was a pearl necklace.. looked antique from the hooks and links…. "Do not say anything about this to anyone – the monkey could have stolen this from someone so until I ask around and find out I will keep it … Next time Mangu shows up you call me son… don't worry you did nothing wrong… saying that dad put the necklace in his pocket and the whole family went back to what they were doing….

Simi got her wheels turning – where could Mangu have got this? I wonder if he has more? Why did he come here? …she kept thinking about these questions and kept writing them down….

The next morning – they all met in the courtyard outside their log cabin there were four other families as they introduced themselves, "Shoemakers, McNaughtons, Lee, Smith and Singh"… 'looks like we have the whole united nations here – commented Singh after the introduction… they had the morning breakfast… and during the breakfast Mr. Singh asked in a subtle way to all of the families if they had lost a pearl necklace…? They all said no..

Anita was their guide for the day – dressed in her camping gear with a compass, a walkie talkie, a pair of binoculars and a first aid kit, she handed a small bag of snacks to Simi and said "you are in charge of this dear…"

The whole family had something in their hand and they went along… as they walked through the bushes and trees, Jot was excited about something he walked over to his papa and whispered in his ear, "Mangu is following us"… Mr. Singh signaled him to keep it a secret… Simi was excited too as Jot showed her Mangu – she waved at him when Anita wasn't watching…. They came across a small stream and rested there for a while…

Simi Dec 11th

When everyone was resting their eyes, Mangu came down and tapped Simi on the back while she was leaning on a coconut tree writing and doodling in her diary. Simi whirled around, only to find that no body was there. She though that it was just her senses tricking her ,but after she turned around , she felt someone or something had threw a round, hard object at her back. She flinched and jumped so high, she touched the leaves on the coconut tree. Simi knew that something had done that, because there weren't any coconuts on the coconut tree she had been resting on.

Simi thought that what ever had done that had to have gone in the jungle. So Simi got her diary and wrote a note to her family, say where she was and why. Then, with her diary, she headed for the jungle. You see Simi was a very courageous girl, so she didn't get scared easily, but the jungle had something that gave her the chills. There were so many trees covering the sun that it was hard for her to see. There were also many vines in the way, but it was a good thing that she had her trusty pocket knife. Simi was taught to always carry a pocket knife with her where ever she went for emergencies. She thought it was very weird to carry it around at the time, but she's glad she did. After about an hour of chopping vines, Simi took a rest on a rock. She thought she was lost as she sat down, but when she did, she felt a flat hard object in her back pocket. When she looked what it was, it was her compass and she was overjoyed to see it there. She used the compass to find her way back to where her family was. By the time she got back, everyone was searching for her. Apparently something happened to the note that she had left them when they were sleeping. The first person to see her was Jot. He was so thrilled to see her, that he gave her a big hug. When they all settled down at the tree, Simi told them what she had done.

While Simi was telling everyone about her adventure, Mangu went to the top of the tree they were sitting by and tried to listen in. At the end Mangu leaned over one of the leaves of the tree and fell down on Jot. Everyone was so surprised that they jumped up. Simi took Mangu and sat him by the tree. Jot asked if Mama and Papa if he could keep the monkey. They said no. Simi secretly wondered if Mangu had stolen the pearl necklace before or if there actually was some sort of treasure on the island of some sort that Mangu knew about. While everyone was returning to the cabins, Simi asked Mangu if he knew if there was some treasure on the island. The monkey nodded his head and pointed to a hole in the tree. Simi looked closer at the hole and noticed there was a crumpled up piece of paper there. Simi pulled it out and saw that it was a ~~treasure~~ map. Papa called them to come because they were leaving. Simi put the ~~treasure~~ map in her pocket, Jot waved good-bye to Mangu, and they ran to catch up to their parents.

When they were back in the cabin, Simi showed the map to Papa. He was so excited to see the ~~treasure~~ map, because he loved having adventures with his daughter. Simi and Papa decided they would keep it a secret until they found the treasure so it would be a surprise for everyone when they found it. Papa tucked the ~~treasure~~ map away and said that next time Simi saw Mangu, to ask the monkey if he knew anything else about the treasure.

Papa said, while Simi did that, he would look on the internet to see if he could find any more information about the treasure.

The Research

Daddy Dec 12th

When everyone was asleep, papa got online – read some emails and replied to some...he then put his hand in his pocket looking for a tissue when he saw the map...

He got excited and started his research... he found out that ... there was a treasure of the Money Pit on the island... man for the past 400 years have been trying to solve this but have not been able to get to the bottom of this pit – whomsoever came close had perished...

This is what he found with his research – stories and theories over the years

The Oak Island Money Pit is the site of the world's longest running hunt for lost treasure.

The Discovery of the Oak Island Money Pit

In 1795 at age 16, Daniel McGinnis made his way across to Oak Island on a fishing expedition.

Once on the island, he found himself stood in a clearing in front of an old oak tree bearing the marks of unnatural scarring. This, he supposed to be caused by a rope and tackle system used to lower material down into a shaft below, indicated by a depression beneath the tree, about 4.8 meters in diameter. This completed the scene as one Daniel immediately recognised from childhood tales of swashbuckling pirates.

The very next day, Daniel McGinnis returned to Oak Island accompanied by two friends, Anthony Vaughan and John Smith. Equipped with picks and shovels they began the task of recover the treasure - but it was to take significantly more digging equipment than first anticipated.

As the three boys began to dig, they found the earth still bore pick marks on its smooth, clay sides. Their excitement rose when, at a depth of 1.2 metres they hit a layer of flagstones. These were removed only to reveal packed logs at 3 metre, 6 metre and 9 metre intervals.

On removing these layers of logs, the boys were quickly realised that they were going to need more substantial tools if they were going to recover the treasure of Oak Island. They reluctantly returned to the mainland, making a pledge to return and recover the treasure.

For hundreds of years, treasure hunters have ventured to Nova Scotia, Canada and tried to recover the treasure which is protected by a series of ingeneous traps. As treasure hunters have attempted to recover the bounty from the Money Pit, cleverly engineered flood tunnels flood the shaft with sea water and a few of them have lost their lives.

Here is the list of theories papa found…

The Jolicure Pit : Acadian treasure

Nova Scotia mysteries: Masonic locations all over Nova Scotia

The Vikings: Vikings make it across the Atlantic to create the Money Pit

Blackbeard : notorious pirate Blackbeard responsible for creating the Money Pit

The British: British Army have created the pit during the American War of Independence

Captain Kidd   Captain William Kidd had buried a hoard of treasure to be found on an island "east of Boston"

Natural formation?   natural sink hole - we look at the evidence.

Freemasons / The Knight's Templar / Rennes le Chateau / Ancient Egypt /

Oak Island's stone formations

William Phips / Sir Francis Bacon

MAP of the island –

"P" marks the PIT

He found an old picture and inscriptions on stones online… he saved them and started to study them.

Forty Feet Below Two Million Pounds Are Buried

These inscriptions translated to **"Forty Feet Below Two Million Pounds Are Buried"** He also found list and pictures of items that have been pulled out of the pit for almost 300 years. Here is the problem papa found out that to hunt for treasure in Nova Scotia, one must hold a valid Treasure Trove License (TTL) issued by the Nova Scotian government.

The next morning he picked up his cell phone and called his attorney and enquired. The attorney assured him that he would do some research and get back to him. Meanwhile papa kept all this a secret and explained to Simi that papa is working on something as soon as he thinks the time is right he would take Simi out to the adventure. He also asked her to not let Mangu out of sight to keep him occupied with fruits and food…

A few days passed and papa got an email back from his attorney.

Dear Mr Singh,

It is true that to hunt for treasure in Nova Scotia, one must hold a valid Treasure Trove License (TTL) issued by the Nova Scotian government. However you are there as tourists and if you stumble upon something you need to turn that over to the Nova Scotian government – historic society.

Kind regards

Eric McMeyer

Attorney at law

Mr Singh was relieved… that evening he sat with the family and shared the island data that he had collected over the past two days. Jot was only happy that he could play with Mangu. Simi was thrilled that they could continue the adventure, but mummy was worried because she heard papa say that almost everyone that got close to the treasure perished. Papa was entrigued that for over 300 years this has been a mystery and they could be a part of this…

Next morning each family was given a walkie talkie and asked to call in every hour to make sure they are fine and that day would be their "OWN DAY". They could sit in their cabins all day or walk around the beautiful island and explore its beauty. The interesting part is that in the past 4 days that everyone was there no one had once mentioned the treasure or money pit. Papa and the family collected their food and necessary items and took off.

The New Journey – A new discovery

The family walked into the woods following Mangu. Papa had the map in his hand the Money pit marked on it but according to his compass Mangu was headed west of the money pit spot. Papa was confused but continued with his family he looked at this watch it had been close to an hour so he called the base and said "this is Mr Singh reporting – all is well". He gave them his location and kept walking. Suddenly Mangu stopped and climbed a tree in a hurry. Papa pushed the family to one side fearing that there was some kind of danger. Mangu was nowhere to be seen – a few minutes later he appeared with a handkerchief with something wrapped in it and threw it at PAPA's feet. Mr Singh picked it up and opened it. He found three bronze, one silver and one gold coin along with a pendant/locket. He stuffed the coins in his pocket and sat down on the rock. The whole family was excited and wanted to see what items were there in the package. Papa just signaled them to be silent and will open the package when they go back to the log cabin in the evening. All excited they walked around for a while and when it started getting a bit dark they decided to go back to the camp. Later in the evening when they were having tea papa called the family to the dining table and said," we will play a little game ", pulled out  the bronze coins and gave them to Simi and Jot – gave mom the silver coin and he had the gold coin and the locket in his hand and said, "I want you all to look at the items and make a note of what you see – I want you all to be a part of this adventure. Simi gave Jot one of the bronze coins and said, "here Jot – tell me what you see…" Jot looked at the coin and said, "I see a monkey sitting down and praying to three people standing with  1818 written … "Simi took a picture of the coin.

Papa looked at the coin and said this is a coin from the East India Company dated 1818 – what is this doing here ? " Simi's coins were similar coins. "Does this mean that this could have some link with England ? UK ? India ? East India company? ". He thought in his mind.

"What do you see in the silver coin ?" he asked mummy – "Well I see a head it says 1820 on it". She replies. Papa  **takes the coin from her hand and looks at it carefully – It's an 1820 British 3 Pence silver coin – WOW…"**

Simi asks her dad,"what do you have ?". "This coin says, King George III 1802.

Good lord all of these coins are from the early 1800's. which means that some one traveling from India / UK stopped here and left these here." "What about the pendant/locket ?" mom asked… "Oh yeah, I completely forgot about that" papa replied as he pulled out the handkerchief from his pocket and laid it on the table. They opened the handkerchief and couldn't believe their eyes. It was a "khanda" a symbol of the sikh community dated back to the early 1800's. Can this be true ? A member of the Sikh community from North West India traveled to this island in the early 1800's and left this here ???

Mr Singh a Sikh himself didn't know what to say.. he carefully collected the items put them back in the handkerchief and put it in his suitcase…. "Let me think what I want to do and not a word to anyone… just act normal"… he instructed his family and they all agreed…

The next morning they woke up took a shower and all assembled in the front courtyard along with the other families.

"I hope you all are having a wonderful time and you have three more days left… today we are going to play a game… you will be given a set of clues to find a hidden treasures in three different stages .. Whosoever finds all the treasures and the final location will be given $100,000… yes you heard us $100,000 however if you don't find anything at all you will have to leave the island today itself… if you are not back by 6:30 PM you will be disqualified…. So you have approx 9 hours to complete 3 stages and find the location of the final treasure. "

Each family was at random given an envelope that contained the following a compass, a knife, a bracelet, and a map. Each family was sent away in different directions.

Mr Singh was a little confused, reason being that he was being sent in the

direction opposite to the location of the "money pit". He could not complain because if he did he would be disqualified. He

looked at Simi and said, " we are here to have fun and fun we will have'. He gave her a high five and walked on their path... he had a map sketched and was tracking the path on the map... After about an hour they had reached the edge of the water and were tired . They all sat and mom pulled out some sandwiches they all were exhausted and didn't want to walk any more. Mom looks over to Simi and asks,"where is Jot ?". "I thought he was with you", she replied..... "Honey is Jot with you ?" she asked Mr Singh. "with me ? no... he was with us but I have no idea"... he replied.. putting down his food they started calling out his name... "JOT ... JOT.... JOT ... where are you ?"

After about 10 mins of shouting – yelling and just getting ready to call the camp they heard a voice,"I am here papa.. what's wrong ? I was with Mangu, he had been following us for the longest time and I have been with him ... he showed me some really cool places.. let me show you..." He replied.... Mom ran over and hugged him ... getting a little upset ... but was glad that he was fine... Father gave him a hug and threw part of the sandwich to Mangu... Simi loved her brother very much and had been crying ... Jot walks up to her and says,"I am sorry Simi.. I promise I will stay with you now... you're the bestest sister in the whole world.." They hugged and laughed.

Jot then took the family near two palm trees that looked like a "X". Mangu showed them a small hole there and he put his hand in there and pulled out a small leather bag, "look papa what Mangu found"... Papa put his hand in and pulled out the contents... he couldn't believe his eyes.... One gold chain and two gold coins ...He pulled out the piece of paper given at the camp it had four things written on it...

One gold chain

Two Gold Coins

One iron Cross with the mark 986 on it.

He crossed the two items and thought to himself.. its only one cross that separates his family and the $100,000. He out the contents back in the bag and gave mangu two bananas.. Jot was happy and so was Mangu. The whole family was happy it was getting a little late and they had about 2 hours to look for the cross.... Mr Singh thought that there is definitely a reason why he was sent this way .. the only way that the camp people would prevent him from winning would be not to have any cross.. and make them return empty handed... the family searched and looked high and low... nothing to be found. Jot asks papa if he can go play in the water.. he agrees and walks with JOT to play in the water... beautiful beach and great clear water.. he just loves it.. mom and simi stayed on the shore ... mangu jumped on the tree and watched them all... While playing Mr. Sing noticed that the sand on the beach the trees and the bushes were all untouched.. like no one has been there for years… well he thought it was strange… he pulls out a plastics ball and throws it over to Jot. Jot throws it back .. they played for about 15 mins and pap calls over to Jot … "Last throw we have to get back then"… he throws the ball Jot misses it and it just floats away… Papa notices.. ball floating away…???? How can a ball float away when the water is still… he notices a small opening between the rocks and the ball floats in there… he signals to his family to stay on the shore and says he will be back…

He pushes aside the rock, pulls out the flash light from his pocket and walks in… doesn't see anything but sea weeds and some floating plants… he keeps walking … in the back of his mind he remembers and thinks he might be close to the cross… he keeps walking after about 50 steps.. he feels like he stepped on something metal. Metal ??? he thinks…. Puts his hand in the water and pulls out a small metal box .. like a jewelry box… he leans on the wall and finds a rock to sit on… meanwhile the family is calling him .. he replies back saying he is fine… constantly looking around to make sure he is safe…. He opens the box and finds a piece of cloth in there with some peebles. He shuts the box and walks out cause he can't really see what was written on the cloth. He walks out to his family who are relieved to see him. Mom says,"forget everything its getting late we need to get back.. its going to be dark." Mr Singh is excited.. he sits in the sand with his family and opens the box and pulls out the cloth. It looks like a few lines drown on them and a place marked X. Now he doesn't know what to do.. puzzling as it may be he knew there was something here that he could of value and history is right in front of him. He tells his family that they are all going to be quite and go back to the camp on time. But they are not going to stay a word to anyone. They all agree and start walking back…Simi was tired papa picked her up… Jot was on mummy's back… they were all walking back…. As they got closer to the camp they heard everyone shouting and singing.. The Shoemakers had won, McNaughton's did get one item but were more interested in just enjoying the island, Lee was busy taking pictures and thought that the competition was just a joke – he was disqualified and was packing his bags to leave the next day, Smith tried hard and collected two of the three things just like Mr. Singh.

Mike, SAM and Anita were on the man made stage – Mike had the mic in hand and handed the cheque for $100,000 to the shoemaker, Mr Singh and Mr. Smith won $1000 but had to return back to the camp what they had found which would then be turned over the historic society for keeping... Mr Singh kept the jewelry box and the cloth with him because technically that was not on the list of things to be collected. They all enjoyed and sang songs all night; they had a huge bonfire with apple cider and marshmallows. The next day was declared as the day you can either explore the island and tour around it on boat or rent a ATV and take your family out. That way you didn't have to walk and can still enjoy the island. Mr Singh chose the ATV .. where they could cruise around the island and see what the cloth map says. He signed up checked out the ATV and was ready to cruise.

At night he contacted Mr Khanna the president of the National Historic Society of India in New Delhi. And explained to him about the items found and where he had seen connection between these items and India and wanted to see if there was any explorer from India who travelled to this part of the world around the early 1800's. Mr Khanna said he would check and email back. Mr Singh hoped that by morning he would get the info and get the "research on its way. Simi wassitting next to him and asked him,"Papa I don't care if you don't find anything .. I am just happy that we are all having fun... I already have 75 pictures in my digital camera... could you pl. upload these and save them on your laptop". Sure he replied.

He sipped on his coffee while he was downloading the pics and was ready to run a slide show when Jot came running and sat in papa's lap saying,"I took some pictures too.. let me see..." They all sat with cups of coffee and soup .. papa set the slide show and they were watching making comments...

"Look look two monkeys... " was Jot's comments,

"Look that is nice the tree and the flowers.. look papa I took that one..." was Simi's comment...

" you look fat in this picture... Simi looks too thin.... Jot what were you doing there... "were normal mom comments.

Hummm… Hummm… were papa's comments… he was looking at the pictures watching everything very closely…

They were all enjoying the show when mom suddenly said … "look look… did you see that ?"
Everyone looked at her confused.. trying to figure out what she was trying to say…
They stopped the show and went back. They saw a picture with Mangu on the track and a fallen tree behind with a pile of old wooden planks….
"where was this" she enquired…
"I donno, but I think that this was close to the water case that is when Mangu got off the tree and was walking on the pathway… " simi clarified…. "OK we know where to go tomorrow…" papa confirmed.

"Can I play with Mangu tomorrow..? can he go with us?" Jot enquired…

" I will pack for the trip .. first aid, supplied, food… " Said mom…. "

I am going to be my papa's right hand and help him with my camera and the research", Simi said saluting to her papa....

"Ok my team we are ready to go have some fun...." PAPA confirmed.

The Family Ventures out

Next morning everyone was ready with their adventure gear and got on the ATV …. Small seats next to the driver where the kids fit well and mom on the other side.. dad driving slow… Simi taking pictures, Mangu on the way waving at Jot … Jot all excited… the perfect start to the adventure the Singh family was looking forward too…

Mr Singh slowed down the ATV when he got close to the "site", he then realized that he was a stone throw distance from the small cave where he found the small jewelry box… Mr. Singh stopped the Atv and looked at Simi,"you ready partner ???? Lets go…" They both walked over to the wooden planks… approx 4 feet long 2 feet wide.. looks like they were broken from a bigger wooden plank..

"Here Simi could you give me a hand with these planks and move them to near the ATV ?" he asked as he handed Simi the small planks…" be careful…".. Simi and papa had taken 4 planks near the ATV .. they found a place where they could lay it down next to each other and se what they have. Mom meanwhile had some sandwiches made and was pouring coffee for everyone…

"Come on over Mr Indiana Jones, eat something before you try to solve the oldest mystery in the world" she said sarcastically…. Dad sat on the grass fired up his laptop to check his emails and took a bite from his sandwich. As he did that the emails were slowly being downloaded… he read the important email deleted spam … as he was doing that he stopped and stared at the screen….

"What happened?" simi Asked… the whole family stared at the screen,,, it was an email from Mr Khanna it read

Dear Mr Singh,

I have no idea how you got the items you sent me pictures off but they seem to be connected to India but all of them being in one place is mind blowing… this is what I have found… The east India Coin – is from Calcutta which is in the easter part of India. The Khanda is a religious symbol of the

Sikh community – a copy of the same Khanda is found on the main door to the Golden Temple in Amritsar Punjab, the holiest of holy shrines for the Sikhs. And the gold King George coin belongs to a Merchant Donald Bradman who traded spices for the for the East India company but lived in Birmingham.

Hoe all these items ended up in the same place – I cannot explain all I can tell you is that looking at the dates and what I have researched is that you need to get some research done on Donald Bradman or his family in UK.

Let me know what you find and how else I can help you …

Sincerely
Mr Khanna
President HIS, New Delhi
"what does this mean ? and how is this going to help us ?" Ask mom…

"Donald Bradman was a merchant which means he was traveling on the sea, He had a crew and someone on that crew was from Punjab and

Calcutta..., which means there is some relation between his ship and this island.. we need to put the pieces of this puzzle together" Mr Singh replied...

As he was busy explaining Simi was looking at the planks and was putting them together to see if they were at one time linked together... along with Jot... she loved putting pieces of the puzzle together .. Jot was helpful but he had Mangu on his shoulder and was busy watching Simi. As she was doing that she asked Jot could you go over to the place where we got these planks from and see if you can find smaller pieces of wood...

"Sure, lets go Mangu", they walked over to the pile of black soil and found a few small pieces of planks Jot gave the pieces to Mangu who took them over to Simi... Simi was putting the pieces together when she yelled out ... "Papa look what I found – ".

Papa put his laptop on top of the duffle bag and walked over to Simi... they stood back and looked at the planks as simi had laid them out ... he could not believe his eyes... the planks had a writing on it it said " ☐ ☐ ▥ ☐ ☐ ☐ ☐ "

East India Company – Donald Bradman – they had just found pieces of the ship that Donald Bradman sailed around 1845 …..

Meanwhile Jot came back crying…" I lost Mangu.." "You lost Mangu what happened…" dad asked…

"I gave him the wood and as he was walking towards Simi …. He fell in a hole over there…, dad please help him he is crying in the hole… please….". Dad rushed to the ATV and pulled out the rope he had brought with him…. And ran to the area where Jot was pointing…. There was a hole about 2 feet in radius and that is all he could see… he took his flashlight and looked in he could see Mangu .. as he got closer the hole widened and he fell in….

Papa…. Simi yelled out and ran to the hole trying to grab on to papa's shirt but fell in with him…. The fall was about 10 feet and there was water underneath… Mr Singh realized that he still had his phone he called his wife – she was hysterical, he asked her to calm down and told her that he would give her a call every 15 mins if he doesn't call then she should call the camp and explain to them what had happened and ask for help...

"Simi is fine I am fine.. don't worry ... I just don't know how lose the rest of the soil is and don't want you in here ...stay up with Jot while Simi and I find a way to get out of here... there is water down here which is coming in from somewhere... we will just try and get to the source and then get out to the place where we found the jewelry box... so calm down.. don't panic.... He explained to his wife...

Mangu, Simi and papa were all underground with a rope, a flash light, a pocket knife, the map and were walking in the direction that they thought the water was coming in from. Papa had the flash light and was shining it on the walls to see if he could find anything there... Simran was scared but felt secure with papa there... mangu was wet and scared too but felt like he was a part of the family and just followed them.

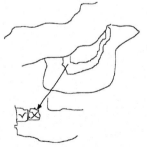

Mr Singh had grabbed a branch on his fall down and was using that as a walking stick to make sure there are no potholes or traps. They walked for about 15 mins and Mr Singh called his wife and hung up signaling that all is well not to worry… he then looked for a handkerchief in his pocket to wipe his face when he found the map in the small jewelry box tucked in his jacket pocket.

He pulled it our sat on a small rock in the cave and was trying to look at it with his flash light … What he thought in the map was the path was actually the underground cave … what he had thought was the big road was actually the water… and to his surprise the "X" mark was actually the small rock that he was sitting on…. He was getting goose bumps and didn't know what was underneath that rock .. he knoew he was close to the water entrance and was safe but didn't know what was under the rock. He took his branch and put it under the small rock to push it aside… he pushed it and managed to move it … he looked at the bottom and was afraid that he might find snales or scorpions… but boldly looked and found nothing…. Nothing at all.. all disappointed he stook on top of the rock and pulled the map out looking at the map he tried to figure out why the "X" was marked there and what was he missing. He couldn't figure it out. Simi and Mangu were watching him didn't know what was going on…

He looked at simi and said,"looks like this is an important locaton where I am standing but can't figure out what it is ". Simi said, "can I help papa".. as she was always willing… "I donno, I am just confused here…."…"Honey we are fine no need to worry I am almost at the end of this cave and getting closer to the mouth of the cave … meet me there " is the message he texted to his wife…he put his arm up in the air in disgust knowing that he is so close but no results… Simi was watching her dad and looked at him feeling sorry for him and said,"its ok papa .. lets go", holding her hand up to help her papa off the rock while he jumped off the rock he tripped and fell in the water…. "You ok papa ?", simi asked. He just nodded and while he was getting up he looks at the roof of the cave right above the rock and sees the "CROSS"… the third item on the list the "CROSS"… He now understood why there was the "X" marked on the map… He said,"Hand me the flash light.. look..do you see what I see? Does that look like a cross to you". Simi nodded her head.

Papa took the branch and tried to get the cross off the ceiling of the cave. It didn't work… he was getting frustrated. Simi, his smart intelligent daughter said,"dad I got a plan… why don't you pick me up let me sit on your shoulder, I will then pry off the cross with the pocket knife we have... I think that will work..what do you think?"... "Good idea.. lady Einstein.. let do it.... " he replied patting her on her back.

He picked her up put her on his shoulder and she tried to dig around the cross. It looked like someone had hammered this into the ceiling. After a few attempts it loosened and fell from the ceiling hitting papa on the head... "you OK papa ?", she asked feeling sorry for him... "Yes I am", he grabbed it as it was falling down.

They walked out of the cave. Jot looked at them and yelled,"look mama there they are, PAPAPAPAPA.. heeeeellloooooooo". Papa looked over and waved with a thumbs up signaling that 'all is well". Papa was picking out sea weeds and dirt off of his clothes... they walked towards mom who was relieved to see them. He pulled out the cross from his pocket and showed it to mom.. she looked at it and said,"a day late or we would have won the $100,000 that the shoemakers won. " She sounded disappointed... Papa looked in her eyes and said,"Honey you have no idea what you have in your hand.... This could be the KEY to the treasure... just keep it... lets have some coffee and head back before its too late…They poured coffee in their mugs had a few sandwiches and relaxed. Meanwhile Mangu found a branch closeby where he sat with his banana that Jot gave him. After a while they got on the modified ATV and were headed back. They got a call from the camp asking everyone to report back immediately. They got to the main camp and found out that the "Smiths" were missing.

"Missing..?? what do you mean missing?" Mr Singh asked. Well they left this morning and haven't heard from them … were worried and would like to get some help from you all… in other words even though its not mandatory – if you still want to help we are going to setup a search party and go look for the Smith family.

Missing - Mr Smith

 This map was shown to the search party... a general idea of what direction the smiths were headed in and the last time the Smiths called in. John Shoemaker was with Mr Singh on the ATV John mentioned that Mr Smith loved the water... " may be he went swimming and sharks got him.", said John... "That's not funny... lets get him and his family back." Replied Mr. Singh... As they got close to the site marked on the map they split the teams and headed in different directions. They were all instructed to inform all if they found and clues... as John/Singh moved towards the beach they saw a duffle bag on the sand with a plastic bag "inflatable raft" written on it... They picked it up and immediately called the rest of the team to get to the beach...
No one was given an inflated raft.. how did Smith get it ?
How did the raft get there ?
Where is the raft ?

Who took it ?

Are the Smiths out in the water ?

All these questions were running through their minds when John saw a red cloth in the water… Mr Singh went towards the water and started swimming towards it. A few mins later he got back… with it .. while he was drying himself Mike looked at the cloth and remembered that Mrs smith had it wrapped around her when the left in the morning… before they left she had stopped by the office to collect the walkie talkies…. He called the camp and asked them to send a jet ski…. While they waited Sam looked at thesearch party and said,"who wants to go…", "I will go … ", Mr. Singh said," just let me go alone – just in case I need to bring them back…"… The team handed him a walkie talkie, a phone, a rope, a small net in case he needed it …. And instructed him to call back every 15 mins to make sure all is well….

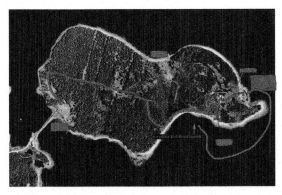

The Jet ski was there and Mr Singh got on it…. But before he left he called his wife and told her not to worry and to keep the kids with the rest of the group... As he was about to leave he saw "MANGU"... Mangu ran up to him and jumped on the Jet Ski... "It's Ok ... It's ok... he is my son's buddy we have known him since we got here"... mangu clung on to Mr. Singh's back and off they went into the deep blue sea.... Mr Singh kept thinking that Mangu is the one who would know this island better than anyone... He was paying attention to his reaction .. moving about the waters slowly looking for clues. He suddenly saw a small tunnel...noticed waves hitting the side of the rock hard over and over..... mangu getting excited... he slowed down and looked there were waves going in and gushing out like there was a flood in the tunnel.... He heard some faint noise from the cave... Mangu jumped off his back and swam to the nearest rock and started jumping up down ... Mr Singh got close to the mouth of the cave and saw the Smith family... "Thank god .." he thought ... I am here don't worry... "hellooooo... helloooo" he yelled... He got close to the rocks threw in the rope and helped the smith family out, he was fighting the waves got thown in the water a couple times but managed to pull himself out and held on to the rope... He finally tied the rope to the top of one of the rocks as an anchor.... Mr smith thanked him and was in tears... apparently .. they were out in the waters just enjoying when the waves pushed their raft towards the tunnel ... not knowing what to do they just clung to each other and drifted... the waves were getting stringer and the problem was that the raft got stuck in the rocks and the family couldn't get out.... Mr Smith was the only one who knew how to swim.. his wife and kids were scared... Mangu wouldn't leave .. he kept jumping up and down over and over again... "come on Mangu .. let go ... " he called him and put his hand out... He called the beach gave them the news, and told them to call his wife to let her know that all is well.

Mangu did not listen... just them Mr Singh thought that Mangu knows this island better than anuone so he asked Mr Smith to hold on to the Jet ski while he climbs on to the rock where Mangu was standing. He got up there and looked inside the tunnel where mangu was looking... the place that Mangu was looking was the opposite side to where the smith family was stuck... he could not believe his eyes... what he saw were two planks set as a cross with a pirate flag ... yes a pirate flag half torn tied on to one of them... He signaled to mangu to quite down and just get to the jet ski... He wanted to get the smith family out to safety first before the tides get stronger... Mr Singh put Mr Smiths son in front of him Mr Mrs Smith and mangu adjusted themselves on the Jet Ski… and rode back to the beach… The people at the beach saw them and were estatic .. the paramedic first aid was there to help.. all the cuts and bruises were being attended too and Mr Singh was the hero…

They got back to the camp and everyone was happy .. the Smith retreated back to their log home.. Mr Singh the hero was treated as well and went back to his log house. After dinner the kids were alsleep and Mr Singh was sipping coffee with his wife when he mentioned the planks and the pirate flag. She was scared when she heard that – "I don't want money, treasure.. nothing .. lets just get out of here… if you would n't have got there in time Mr smiths would have been in trouble… I don't want to to go there again… I DON'T CARE ..". She firmly replied…

Tie up the loose ends…

Mr Singh didn't know what to say. He had work to do. He got online answered to his emails and laid down in bed thinking what to do next… The next logical thing to do would be to tie the lose ends and see if really there is something to look for or its just a wild goose chase…

He went to the living room and laid down on the floor opened his laptop and started laying out the things in order…

The 1st present that Mangu gave

The pouch they found with the coins

The link to British Empire and the link to India and the Sikhs

The map in the underground cave in the jewelry box

The CROSS from the cave

The two planks with the pirate flag

As he listed these and was pondering over them….. when he heard footsteps… for a second he was scared… he turned back and he saw.."SIMI, what are you doing here this late ?".

"Papa I couldn't sleep can I sit here for a while please...." She asked...

"Sure .. may be you can help me with this mess..." he said comforting her

She was happy , always willing to help papa... she sat next to him and looked at all of the things he was writing ....

"Ok what do you think"... he asked her...

'Lets see... hummm..", with her right hand scratching her head, thinking like she was really intrigued..

"papa the planks you saw in the tunnel did you see anything written on them???" she asked...

"No, they were quite far .. but good question... I never thought of that... he made a note of it. "What else do you see Simi" he asked

"Well if I was the pirate and I had things hidden I would not hide them in one place .. I would spread them out so if someone finds my treasure I will still have some left..". She said intelligently…

"Good Job.., simi You know what I like the way you think tomorrow you and I are going to go out and see if we can find some more clues, its getting too late now.. you need to get back to bed, I'll go tuck you in"… saying that he walked in with her and tucked her in… on his way back he was thinking that what Simi said was right….

He wrote the following on a piece of paper…

Check….Writings on the planks in the tunnel…

The 1st present that Mangu gave

The pouch they found with the coins

The link to British Empire and the link to India and the Sikhs

The map in the underground cave in the jewelry box

The CROSS from the cave

The two planks with the pirate flag

The next day they woke up and joined the festivities in the front court yard... Mr Smith walked over to Mr Singh and said," Mr Singh thanks again for helping my family out ... I am a pretty laid back man and not a very adventures type.. I want you to have this..."... saying that he handed mr Singh a small pouch, "I found this in the tunnel tucked between the rocks.. I am not sure its value but its worth a lot less than our lives you saved... thanks again...." Mr Singh put it in his pocket to avoid attention... he them walked over to his log cabin and opened the pouch... What he found in there was absolutely astounding... it was a coin and old coin....

Simi walked in as he was looking at the coin, she was there to get her papa for breakfast they were serving outside...

"look Simi what Mr Smith gave me...." He said showing her the coin..

"Cool a "Mayan Calender"...." She exclaimed...

"A what ????.. Mayan Calender, how do you know ?" he asked her...

"We are learing this in Ancient History Mr Gonzales our History teacher has been talking about this for almost a week… I can see this in my sleep papa… and you know something interesting 2010 and 2012 is supposed to be a very interesting year in this calendar…. Mr Gonzales said that 1000's of years ago they had said that the world would end in 2012 and the only way to avoid that was if in year 2010 – 100's of year old mystery was resolved"… as soon as she said that they both looked at each other like they had just seen a ghost and were in disbelief.

"Are you thinking what I am thinking " .. papa asked…

"Oh boy.. I donno papa kind of exciting and scary…".. saying that she shrugged her shoulder – "donno.. what to do…"

"OK… now we got the mayan calendar on my list too… how many people have been here and what all is on this island that no one has found that is falling in my lap.."… he said looking at his list and had planned that after dinner he would make an excuse take simi with him and head out - he had the map of the island and had marked all of the trips and finding on it…

They walked out and joined the group, had their breakfast. Mr Singh acted like nothing was wrong and like nothing had happened...

When done he looked at his wife and said," I am just going to take Simi for a small trip.. around the island.."

She looked at her husband and said, " I know what you are upto ... but take care and be carefull"

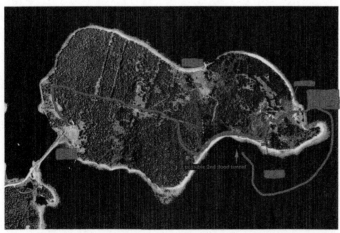

"what's the matter honey ?" He asked her...
"We wonder too - how many different coins are going to end up on the island? Who was there? Will you and Simi

have to go on another wild chase to find all the places the pirates hid their treasures? Will you have to give them up to the government? Will you get a finder's fee? So many things we that worry me I find out!" she said… squeezing his palm….

"Don't worry mummy we will be fine, just think that papa and I are going to go out and have some fun and see if we can find some answers. If not then no problem if we do that would be a lot better now wouldn't it ?... plus you have Jot who can read you all facts and figures from the almanac he brought with him…Don't worry I will make sure papa doesn't get stuck any where keep you phone on…" She said hugging her mom tight as she could.

She handed him the regular travel bag and waved goodbye…
This was the map in hand and this is what they were going to use for the travel….

Mr Singh was the adventurous type and now he had a daughter who was with him to help him out…

"Papa, why don't we follow the trail to where you found Mr Smith, where the tunnel was flooded … I had it marked here ".. Simi asked her papa…

"That's where we are headed…., just make sure you remind me that every 30 mins we call mom and let her know that all is well ok ?" Mr Singh replied…

"Ok papa.. will do.. no problemo.."… Simi promptly replied to her father as they zoom passed the beautiful shoreline … They were enjoying the sight when Simi yelled out, " papa look… look…" pointing out in the direction of the shore line there was a piece of pipe sticking out… Dad slammed on the brakes and rode right to the pipe sticking out…. "What could this be ? ", he asked his daughter .. " I donno ??".. she replied

He looked carefully it was rusted… he picked up a rock and started hitting the top of the pipe cap. To loosen it up. Finally he got it off and a small snake slithered out ..." HOLY SMOKES"... he yelled pushing his daughter back and getting away from the pipe... The snake slithered away "Simi.. just think if the lid was ON tight how did the snake get in ??? Looks like there is an opening at the other end"

Mr. Singh had read about people trying to drill on the island to get some hint about the treasure... "Hand me the rope.." he asked simi... "She ran to the ATV and got the rope... he tied a rock to the rope and while he was doing that simi asked,"papa what if there are more snakes..." Don't worry simi just run if you see one"... and smiled at her. He knew the rope was about 100 ft... he kept lowering the rope.. Looking at Simi.. kept lowering it... after lowering it for about 90 feet he looked disappointed and started pulling the rope back up... when he pulled it out he stood up and was wrapping the rope on a wheel ... without paying attention to the rope and just looking over the shore line admiring it when simi yelled out "papa look... look at the rock".... He turned around and couldn't believe it .. it was soaked in some sort of oil....... "Oil ???? ".. he exclaimed and smelled the oil... its motor oil, burnt motor oil... where did it come from? He thought...

"what are you thinking papa ?"... she asked her papa... "Donno simi... donno what to do.... Why is there oil at the bottom of the pipe ? how come the snake that jumped out did not have oil on it ? who drilled this hole ? and what could be at the bottom ?... how do we get to the bottom of the pipe ? too many questions not enough answers dear..."... he said with a big question on his face.

"I donno papa but if I were you .. I would write this in my diary mark this spot and move along further towards the planks ..., oh yeah and lets not forget to call mummy "... she replied.. she called her mom and told her all was well. Her Papa signaled her not to tell mama anything... As soon as the talk was done they made a note of the place... and Mr Singh then looked at his daughter and said,"I have a gut feeling that there was something going on here through this pipe.. I have an idea... lets go to the pipe...".

He opened the lid of the pipe and Mr Singh tied the rock back to the rope and let it down the pipe to about 95 feet and let it hang there.. he tied the top to the top of the pipe...

pushed the lid shut and made a note of it. He looked at her and said"you never know what we might find… let s go…"

He wanted Simi to keep all of this a secret of what had happened there and rode off on the ATV towards the plank area. As they got close to it Mr Singh parked the atv away from the small cliff and walked towards the edge. "Careful papa" ..

He found a pathway leading down to the water, the water had calmed down. Simi followed him to the edge of the water.

"Ok Simi I am going to tie this end of the rope to my belt and the other end to this rock… I want you to wait here … don't go anywhere jus sit tight and keep this walkie talkie handy.. if this bell I have at the end of the rope starts ringing a lot then call for help immediately … I will be careful don't worry…"… he said that and tied the bell to the rope and the rope to the rock. And got into the water… the water was knee deep for most of the way and started getting deeper, Simi watched her dad and was a bit worried.. she was stretching to keep an eye on him until she couldn't see him. She then checked the walkie talkie and called mom to let her know on what was going on. Mom did not want to alert anyone but she kept the phone and the walkie talkie with her. She knew that the phone was with dad and the walkie talkie with Simi. She also knew that dad wouldn't try anything stupid and was just the adventurer type but unexpected accidents could have grave consequences.

Simi was waiting with her hands as she was praying to god that dad would come back and not hear the bell. Meanwhile dad walked and walked slow and steady toward the planks. He walked to the planks and saw that the pirate flag was an old one all tattered and torn... he tried to pull it off the plank and both the planks can crashing down.

Simi heard the splash and called out to her dad... he heard her and answered back... "I am fine don't worry...." He pushed the planks aside and in the water he felt like he was standing on a step.. He set the planks on the rock an took a picture… he then bend down to see what "step he was standing on… it was a flat rock that felt like a step. He used the plank to prop them or try and move them. He pushed hard nothing moved. He was confused. Well, a bit disappointed he waited and sat on the rock for a while and kept staring at the plank… the then realized that the planks were off of one plank… so if he put them together it would be one plank… but then thought way would someone break this plank to make two pieces and leave them there.

There has got to be a reason. He got up from where he was sitting and started to look around with his flashlight… As he was looking around he had one of the planks in his hand with which he was tapping onto the walls of the tunnel. And trying to figure out the puzzle… as he was tapping the plank got stuck in one of the crevices in the wall… he looked close and found out there was a similar crack about 3 feet to the right of where the plank was stuck… he stretched out and reached out to the other plank. Grabbing the plank he put it in the other crack… now he was standing with planks in both his hands, the flashlight in his headband flashlight holder and just like Indiana Jones he pushed both of the planks in their respective cracks and let out a cry,"Bolle ... So nihal...... Sat sri akal...". As he did that the rock slipped out and fell in the water. It was a 3ft block that fell in the water. He stepped forward and pulled off the flashlight from his headband and tried to look in... he couldn't see much, just water at the bottom... didn't know what to do.

He was very curious to see because of the whole thing that the planks fit the block and the fact the planks would have been there to push this block out ... who so ever put it there would have put it there so the next time they come there it would be easy for them to push the block out. He was exhausted and tired he knew that Simi and the rest would be worried sick... so he picked the block up carefully pushed it back in its place and walked back out to where Simi was waiting. As soon as Simi saw him she was relieved....she gave him a hug, called mom on the walkie talkie and had mom and dad talk. They were all glad. Mr Singh sat on the rock with Simi pulled out a water bottle and explained to Simi everything that happened in the tunnel. She couldn't believe it and said,"Papa I am coming with you ... I am not going to let you go back I am coming with you...". He knew that his daughter cared about him and was saying that but he also knew that she was the adventures one and wanted to be with dad.

The Team proceeds…

As soon as he was done with the water and a small sandwich he said, "lets go kiddo… lets see what we find". Saying that he walked towards the block. As the water got deeper he picked simi up and slowly they got to the block.. He did what he did before and pulled the block off. Simi was thrilled and curious… the hole was big enough for simi and papa to go in one by one… they walked in into the tunnel and kept walking slowly.. both of them flashing their flash light and slowly the tunnel ceiling got higher and higher. Until they entered a room with only wet floor no water and a much cleaner room … there were some old chairs and planks… they both looked at each other. As they mover forward they heard a voice "WELCOME MR. SINGH… and SIMI .. we have been waiting for you"… They were shocked to hear that they turned around and saw "SAM, MIKE and ANITA all three standing there with revolvers in their hand…"

"You were waiting for me ?" he said raising his hand over his head and simi clinging to her dad

"Yes we were .. we have been watching you, we have been keeping an eye on you and guess what our spy has been with you all this time… say hello to MANGU"…. Mike said pulling Mangu from the side rock…

"Holy macro, " Singh explaimed….

""Yes we send him there to you cabin .. we gave him the pouch with the coins … we lead you to all the places .. but we never knew you would be so smart to get this far … we need something that you have … NOW… hand it over to us .. don't force us to shoot you .. you hand it over and we will partner with you in what ever we find … you don't we will have to finish you…" Said Anita

"What do I have that you need ?" Singh was confused…

"The cross".. we have been looking for the cross for over 10 years and couldn't find it .. we never knew where it was… so we send mangu to you and you found it for us… we need that "… Mike explained…

"The cross.. " Simi and papa looked at each other…

"Yes the cross don't act so dumb" we had this camera implanted in Mangu … that no one knew.. he was in the cave with you when you found the cross we had seen it but never knew how to get it from you without raising hell… so let us have it and what ever we find we will split is 4 ways … " SAM explained…

"OK.. " Mr Singh said… and thought how can I trus these guys but he had no choice…

"you will have to come with us, and help us because it is a known fact that who so ever would find the cross would be the only one to get to the treasure…"

"ok Mr Singh knew that there was no need to fight them but better to join hands…"Simi come on lets go".. he held his daughters hand and walked with Mike, SAM, Anita and Mangu…

They walked for about 10 mins and the phone rang…

"Hello Honey where are you ?", asked Mrs Singh,

"Fine dear.. just taking care of stuff" he replied… looking at Mike holding a gun…

Mrs Singh knew exactly that there was something wrong… "taking care of stuff" was their personal code for "I am in trouble – send for help". She then went over to the main hut for help and found out that Mike, SAM and Anita were missing … which was unusual because normally atleast two of the three were always there…

She then had a hunch that there was something wrong with this picture… she rushed back to her
Hut and pulled out her personal latop she plugged it in and once fired up she pulled out a USB device and plugged that in while Jot was watching her. In a few mins the screen went blank and there came up a map of the island with a light beeping. "OH so that's where they are", she said to herself. She asked Jot to get his coat and asked him to be quite and not tell

anyone where they are going. She went next door saw an ATV sitting there and requested if she could take her son in for a ride…

She got on the atv with a bag pack that had her laptop and some stuff she had brought in with her. Jot was all excited. As soon as he got on the ATV she whispered in his ear "get ready son we are going to have fun – some bad guys have got papa and Simi we are going out to get them" – they high fived each other and off they were headed in the direction of the beep.

She had a wrist watch with a 3"X3" square screen… this was picking up signals from her laptop in her bag. She drove for a while and got to the point where Simi and pap's tracks stopped. She pulled the watch close to her face and gave her co-ordinates – walked down the tracks and Jot followed her all excited and was wondering what mummy was doing… She kept looking at her watch and kept following the beep. She found the hole in the wall pulled out her 9mm and strapped a swiss knife with blade out to jot's ankle. She then explained to him. "son we are going in you are a brave boy don't be scared and use this when someone tries to hurt you ok… but make sure you look at me before using it .. ok beta…?"

He puts his hand up in the air and says," I am not scared mom – I am with you" don't worry I have seen papa use this and know its not a toy I will keep an eye on you … lets go get papa and simi " giving her thumbs up

She walks into the room and keeps the gun close to her body – ready to shoot… She could see her husband…

Meanwhile…
Mr Singh and the team walked about 20 feet in front of Mrs Singh and jot. Not knowing that they were behind – suddenly there was a small vibration in Mr Singhs wrist watch. They had a transmitter when both turned on and were within 15 feet of eachother they would vibrate. Mr Singh smiled to himself and knew that Mrs Singh was somewhere close. But he wouldn't dare say that and reveal it all. He just followed the team they walked through passages, climbed down a bunch of dirt steps dug underground and ended up in a small underground room. Singh figured it was atleast 150 feet from where the atv was parked… Anita looked at Mr Singh and said"THE CROSS PLEASE"… HE handed her the cross… she pulled out one from her pocket took the other one from Mr Singh and instructed Mike

to tie Mr Singh and Simi to the rock. She walked in alone to the two man made cross indents in the wall and placed the two crosses – as soon as she did that the ceiling crashed – a rock from above her crushed her and a rope ladder dropped down – SAM and Anita were killed on the spot. Simi screamed and was scared.. "don't look beta – don't worry.
There were only three left – MIKE – Mr Singh and Simi.
Mr Singh looks at Mike," wanna untie us and we can work on this together" – leave me tied here and you are on your own… - Mike feels threatened and puts aknife to mr Singhs throat,"all of this happened because of you – I lost my friends I am going to hurt you so baad that you will regret you ever came to this island…" he made a small cut in his arm…
As soon as he did that he heard a voice and felt a gun to his head,"Drop it or I will shoot, swear to god I won't think twice…." Mike dropped his knife… Jot ran up to Mr Singh and cut the rope with his knife…before he did that he looked at mom and she nodded her head.

The whole family tied Mike down with his own rope and made sure it was secure. "How did you find me ?" Mr Singh looked at his wife…

"Come here simi " – you see these earings these are not normal earrings these have a tracking mechanism in them which I can track from my laptop and have that tracked on my wrist watch. I made sure that whenever Simi left with you I had them activated and knew where you were. She pulled out an ID from her pocket and said – "Agent 1824-hawthon – CSIS - **Canadian Security Intelligence Service** – "

The Truth is reveled...

Jot, Simi and Singh – their Jaws dropped....

"Sorry I was sworn to secrecy – Had I reveled this I could have endangered my family" I have been with the secret service for the past 5 years working undercover – we have reason to believe that the drug dealers have been using this island to move money and drugs – the whole trip was pre planned." –

Jot, Simi and Mr Singh could still not get over the shock that the lady who would wrap her kids up in 4 layers of clothing in cold – sun screen in ever summer trip – watching and tasting every food the kids ate is s secret agent....

They looked over at Mike and mike was equally shocked. Mr Singh patted him down and emptied his pockets.. two knives – about $5000 in cash... a cell phone... a pack of cigarettes and some loose change... He was clean.

"What do we do now Ms 1824 Hawthorn – ' " He asked...

Well 1st we get on this ladder and see what's at the other end – I have signaled for backup which probably is waiting for us…

They walked towards the ladder and mom climbed up slowly – before she did that she tugged on it just to make sure that its firm and sturdy – they decided that one adult two kids then the last adult will climb…

Mrs Singh went up first – followed by Jot and Simi – Mr Singh followed them. Once they all got up there mom lit a portable flame she pulled out of her bag that would stay lit for about 30 mins – they place was more like a man made loft carefully constructed and hidden from everyone – Mr Singh went back to the ladder and pulled it up – he rolled a boulder to cover the spot so no one could come in –

Mrs Singh handed her husband and kids one portable flame "as soon as we see this one going out we light the next one"… She moved forward towards the small source of light through the rocks.

The family followed her… Simi and Jot all excited and nervous. They walked a few steps and suddenly Mrs Singh stepped on a lose rock and the bottom fell … luckily Mr Singh was holding on to her hand and pulled her back… they could see a dark hole but no end … both looked at each other… this hole was big enough for an adult to slide through but nothing to hold on to … no idea what was there…

Meanwhile the backup that Mrs. Singh had signaled was on the island and had tracked down to where Mike was tied up… he was found DEAD… Apparently he was afraid that no one would find him – he panicked and had a massive heart attack. The search team hauled all the bodies out and walked around to see if Mrs. Singh was there. She was nowhere to be found. The team decided they would walk back to the camp and look for her there.

The CODE……

Mr and Mrs Singh collected ever pc of rope loose clothing and tied it all together approx 50 feet. Tied a rock to one end and lowered the rock into the dark hole… - kept lowering it .. and lowering it … it finally hit bottom with about 5 feet left…. They pulled is back up and to their surprise 3 feet of the rope was dipped in water… so there was a way out… but who goes 1st and how safe is it down there ???? Mr Singh goes 1st followed by the kids and the Mrs Singh is what they decided.

They tie the rope to the rock near their feet and mr Singh kisses his kids and slides down slow … slow and very carefully… armed with nothing but a pocket knife. After a few mins he hits the water – slowly slides down into the water – its dark very dark

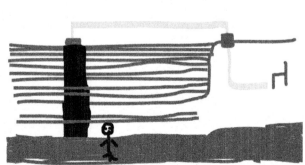

he pulls out his mini flash light and looks around... The signal to get the kids down was to tug hard on the rope – he kept looking around to see if there was any danger in getting his family down... A few fish and aquatic animals nothing dangerous... but he was trying to figure out as to why was this shaft there.... This is what he sketched   water was flowing to his right.... He knew there was some sort of a passage to his right he kept walking in that direction and saw a "X" mark on the wall he tried to push it and it did get pushed in and opened up a small hole in the wall ... meanwhile the family was worried so he rushed back to the rope and gave it a TUG.... One by one his family was down in the water with him ... they walked up to the spot – pushed the "X: and a small hole in the wall opened up that contained a silk cloth with a note that said...☐

1856 - You are the 1st to find this box - all the treasure has been moved - Here is the code

[encoded cipher text]

☐ ☐

Mr Singh slowly wraps up the silk cloth and walks towards the light.. after walking for a few minutes they come over to a large boulder through which the source of light was seeping through. They tried to push the boulder together and just managed to shift it a bit.. Rested for about 15 minutes... Went at it again and after about 45 mins of pushing and resting they managed to push the boulder to squeeze through...

As soon as they were out they all hugged each other and Mrs Singh signaled the backup team with her co-ordinates.. in 10 minutes there were two speedboats speeding towards them. With blankets and hot coffee they were seated in the boat. While waiting for the boat Mr Singh had a talk with the kids and told them not to whisper a word to anyone of what happened...

They were taken back to the camp. Informed that there was a tragedy and they all had to leave. Mr Singh and his family were aware of the tragedy but didn't whisper a word to anyone. They flew back home – Toronto.

Mr Singh's family had a great adventure and a key to probably the greatest wealth on earth hidden for over 300 years and an unsolved mystery. Kids got back to their school work after a while. Mrs Singh and Mr Singh both wanted to decipher the code but didn't know how. And didn't know that even telling someone could be a problem... so they just kept the silk cloth and decided that they would both work on it. They contacted their friend in India : Mr Khanna the president of the National Historic Society of India in New Delhi. Mr Khanna was not told the whole story but knew there was something important that Mr Singh had and advised him to fly down to Ned Delhi. Mr Khanna picked him up and Mr Singh pulled out a piece of paper at the office : handwritten he had the following :

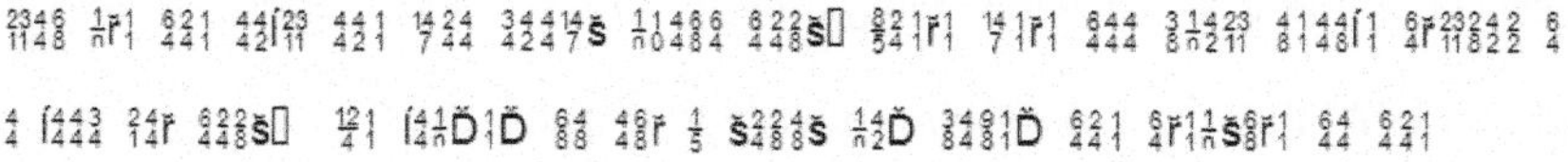

[handwritten coded text]

"Here is what we found.. I need help and I don't want too many people knowing about this – cause except for my family you are the only one who knows about this.." Singh said worried about what would really come out of this.

"Well the only way we can do this is if you and I both start work on this immediately – cause this looks like a mathematics code that needs to be deciphered, normally used by old pirates who knew this language... Most of them used this code to communicate to make sure that the loot is well protected. Unfortunately this code is not that well documented but lets see what we can do. Sleep well tonight we will start 1st thing in the morning - I will send a car pick you up tomorrow "..this 75 year old Mr Khanna replied with confidence and concern.

The next morning Mr Singh was picked up met with Mr Khanna. I have two samples of these letters I got from my visit to London a few years ago. Here they are – which were deciphered and that is the only thing we can use…

[encoded ciphertext]

Translated to :

we traveled across the globe and found great adventures we have seen great wealth in india we found gold coverd thrones and streets paved with silver coins

ψουρ ωορλδ ισ ινχομπλετε ψουρ σηιπσ αρε εμπτψ ιφ ψου ηαϖε νοτ τραϖελ εδ το 4 χορνερσ οφ τηε ωορλδ ☐ τραϖελ το τηε νεω ωορλδ ανδ ψου ωιλλ φιν δ τρεασυρεσ τηατ ηαϖε βεεν στορεδ φορ μανψ ψεαρσ

Translated to:

…your world is incomplete your ships are empty if you have not traveled to 4 corners of the world – travel to the new world and you will find treasures that have been stored for many years…

Mr Singh and Mr Khanna worked on this and finally after days of checking references and using the two notes this is what was the final result:

you are the only one who knows about this. There were too many people trying to look for this. We loaded up our 4 ships and moved the treasure to the

So Mr Singh puts the note together and this is what showed up -
In English : 1856 - You are the 1st to find this box – all the treasure has been moved – Here is the code
CODED : you are the only one who knows about this. There were too many people trying to look for this. We loaded up our 4 ships and moved the treasure to the

When put together :

1856 - You are the 1st to find this box – all the treasure has been moved – Here is the code you are the only one who knows about this. There were too many people trying to look for this. We loaded up our 4 ships and moved the treasure to the

It was 2 AM in the morning when Khanna and Singh put this together... As soon as that was put together they looked at each other and started sweating... what do I do next thought Mr Singh – should I show Mr. Khanna the rest of the note or should I just try and decipher this myself...? I will sleep over this and then decide..

He looked at Mr Khanna and said," OK... this is all I got... may be the other half of the note is still on the island... next visit I will see what we can do about this... ". He paid Mr Khanna Rs10,000 for the help and next day flew back to Toronto... Not once did he mention anything to his wife – he wanted to show her this and make sure she is in with him.

The Plot Thickens...

All through the flight Mr Singh was thinking of what to do next – his plan was to share this information with his family, try and decipher the code and then see if there is any light at the end of the tunnel. He gets down at the Toronto airport and looks out for his family – they were not there… may be they are stuck in traffic is what he thought and got a cab and was headed home. He had picked up a small doll for his daughter, a stuffed baby elephant for his son and a hand crafted jewelry set for his wife. Smiling all the way he got home. When he got to the front door and opened it he was SHOCKED !!! the whole place was ransacked… he called for his family – no answer… he called the cops immediately – they were there in minutes… the whole place was crawling with cops dusting the place for fingerprints. Just then the school bus stopped by the house and Simi ran to the house.. when she got closer she was scared to see the scene.. Mr Singh walked up to her and hugged her.. "don't worry Simi.. all is well…"…

The cops spent about 3 hours dusting for fingerprints took them back to the lab and Mr Singh called for a team to come and put his house in order – when all was set it was about 9 pm Mr Singh called his sister Roseline she came with her daughter roshline. He ordered pizza and narrated the whole story to Roseline. Roseline was shocked. And tried to comfort her brother

– "don't worry I will take Simi with me to my place until we figure out what happened to Jot and her mom". As she said that Mr Singh pulled out a piece of paper from his pocket that he had picked up when he 1st entered the house it said

☐ Ωε ηαϖε ψουρ φαμιλψ ☐ γιϖε υσ τηε χοδε ☐ φυλλ χοδε ανδ ψου χαϖε τηεμ βαχκ ☐ ωε προμισε ωε ωιλλ χαλλ ψου☐

Roseline a Master in languages translated the note : "We have your family – give us the code – full code and you can have them back – we promise-- we will call you".

She looked at Mr Singh and said,"this looks like an east European dialect and needs is spoken in the Serbia area among the mountains where they have religious monks and priests residing, they have a sect who speaks this language amongst themselves only – the only way you can interact with them is by truly responding to them – they are known to be ruthless and have been hiding in the mountains for over 800 years… - now we just have to wait "

Mr Singh saw Simi and her cousin playing and eating pizza – he asked simi to pack a few clothes and go with her aunt – meanwhile he asked his sister to keep her phone besides her so he could link her in when they call. Mr Singh bid simi goodbye and went back to his den and sat there staring at the note and thinking …

Who are these people ?

Where is my family ?

How did they know about the code ?

Cause the only person who had knowledge about the code was his wife, his kids and Mr. Khanna..MR KHANNA !!!! holy Toledo.. what if he leaked it out ? he was the only outsider who had some info about the code… but we have known him for years why would he do such a thing? And if I call him now that would alert him… So I need to lay low and try and get this resolved…

He fell asleep on the recliner around 2 AM – the phone rang – the number on the caller ID did not look familiar he answered the phone and immediately got his sister on the other line.

"So Mr Singh, what have you decided? Co-operate and get your family back – don't co-operate and you will be sorry"

"I am the only one with the code if you harm my family no one in your 6 billion population will ever know the code.. so I call the shots here... I want you to get my family on the phone – I want them to be safe and in good hands – I would prefer a four or five star hotel. Once that is confirmed we will talk... I will co-operate but won't let you walk all over me" Mr Singh firmly replied.

"You are trying to drive a hard bargain but I see you do make sence – well here talk to your wife and they will be moved to a safe location and be taken care off... once that is done I will call you again..."

"Hello.. hello.. hi dear .. how are you ?" Mr Singh inquired..
"I am fine.. Jot is fine... no problem.. Ihave no.... " this is all Mrs Singh could get in.

"You heard her she is fine… I will call you…once we are ready - talk in about 12 hours…" The phone was slammed…

Roseline was still on-line with Mr Singh – " don't worry… let me know when they call…"

Mr Singh is happy that the family is fine. He knows that until he has the code he will be able to dictate his terms but on the same side he didn't want these people to have the code. He spend the sleepless night thinking about what he needs to do – he finally falls asleep. Next morning he woke up getting ready to go to the office and he gets the call. "Meet us at the corner of "Main and Stewart at 1 PM sharp. A blind singer at that corner would have a donation box in front of him put the code in there – we will then at 2pm release your family. If there is a problem you need to take care of it. Needless to say that informing the police would be stupid." – and they hung up the phone…

Mr Singh had already linked his sister in the call. "As soon as I drop the kids off to school I will be there – don't worry". Rosline said.

Mr Singh, immediately called the office and got a briefing of what is going on and said he would be late.

He puts a handwritten copy of the code – on a paper and put it in his pocket... got in his car at 12 headed downtown when he gets a call.... "Mr. Singh this is Stuart little – I am Agent 5959 Barr with CSIS – I used to work with Agent 1824 Hawthorn – I need to talk to you in person – slow down your car and take the next exit 89 stop at the 1st gas station to the right park your car and go to the rest room." Mr Singh follows his directions takes the next exit off of the highway and parks at the pump. Asks for where the restroom was at and walked towards the restroom. There was a sign on it saying :OUT OF ORDER" Casually looking around to make sure he is not being followed. He walks into the restroom not knowing what to expect – turns around and locks the door. As soon as he does that **"CLANG"** the bottom falls and Mr Singh drops down about 10 feet. He gets up from the ground dusting himself it was dark with a small bulb in a basement room of about 10 feet X 10 feet. "Welcome"... he hears a familiar voice but too dark to recognize it. As the figure walks towards Mr Singh he notices that there is a lady and a man. When they get closer to him he is absolutely shocked..... it is "Mr Khanna and Rosaline".

The Conspiracy...

April 28, 2011

He almost falls down... can't believe what he sees..."what on earth are the two of you doing ?"... he asks...

"What are we doing ?... are you nuts ??? with millions at stake here you think we don't get our share ?"... Mr Khanna replies

"Ok lets discuss that later.. first of all where is my wife and son"

"They are with Alex..., don't worry they are perfectly safe... your story leaked out and they want their cut actually we want it all" Roseline replied

"What do you mean WE ?", Mr Singh asks...

"Don't act dumb..." Mr Khanna replied...,"I called Rosaline as soon as you left – I was on the next flight myself, it was her idea... we have our own little team in Europe that looks for artifacts that are rare and we steal them... we then have them auctioned through our museum in india to make it look legit... Since I am the top dog there no one questions me and I have access to all unsolved mysteries and people that spend their life time looking for them ... I have a database of people who in the past 200 years have tried to solve this... Now you have the code hand it to us and you get your family back..."

"But you are my sister…Rosaline" Mr Singh said…

"Yes that is why they haven't killed you …, I am not kidding the word is out and if the Italians find out I won't be able to help you…, you are family and yes I will help you .. right now I am helping you by keeping the family alive… next I will help you get a cut from the treasure.. we still need to decipher it and see if its true or justa wild goose chase…"

Mr Singh knows that his sister will do what is good for the family she has always been a good sister… he pulls a copy of the code out of his pocket and hands it to Mr Khanna. Mr Khanna – looks at Mr Singh and says… ,"you can go now"…

"What where is my family what about them ? helllloooo…"… Mr Singh yells at him…

Overhead door opens – a ladder is dropped down… while Mr Singh looks at that there is another door behind him through which mr. khanna disappears…

Mr Singh jumps at him to find out about his family ….but he is gone..
Rosline disappears too… Well he has no choice but to get on the ladder

and walk to his car... He does that and is shocked again... - His wife and his son are in the back seat....

"Thank god" he says that hugging his family.... As he was doing that the phone rings..."Hope you are happy now... I will drop Simi at your place in 20 mins.. take your family and just disappear to Nabha... no one will find you there.." it was Rosaline... His wife hands him an envelope with four tickets to Bombay... He rushes home.. Simi is out there in the front yard playing with the neighbor kids...

Mr Singh rushes in picks up what he can and they are off to the airport... A 24 hour flight and they were in Bombay... he calls his friend who picks them up... They take the train to Nabha and finally they are safe... His uncle there happy to see them and gets a house for them with servants, a car and a chauffeur. In a few days he finds out that there is a British School about 10 kms away.. he gets his kids in school there and life goes on... he starts a small computer cyber café calls his partner in Canada and tells him to take care of business he would be out for a while for personal reasons.

One evening he was sitting in his living room looking out and sipping tea… His wife walks up to him sits next to him and feels sorry for him.. "In a few weeks our life has turned upside down.. don't worry dear… the code, the map everything wasn't ment to be…"

"Ramu, get me my black diary …" Mr Singh calls his servant.
Mr Singh takes the diary and shows her a trail of events … she keeps looking at him feeling sorry… once he is done he puts his hand on her head and pats her trying to tell her not to worry and pulls out a hair pin from her hair… she is taken back… He puts that hair pin in the corner of the black diary and cuts off the corner where a piece of cloth sticks out… he slowly pulls is out … IT IS THE ORIGINAL CODE – right in his hand….
"But you gave them the code.. what good is this to us now" She asked…
"That's what you think and that's what they think… I stayed up all night and deciphered the code.. I then created a new code for them to get my family back… so they are out there on a wild goose chase… we are safe sipping coffee once things settle down.. we go out there and rightfully get what "FATE" had in store for us…"

Mrs Singhs eyes light up.."good lord...., I know there was a reason why I married you but this is tooooo much... I quit my job thinking I was the only smart detective – you are two steps ahead of me..."

"Just sit back and relax.. enjoy your coffee tomorrow I will show you the real code and what it ment.... Life is like a box of chocolates... ahhahahaha" He laughs hard and hugs his wife...

The Code finally revealed….

The next day as his kids get back from school and they are done with dinner.. he sits with his wife in the study and pulls out the documents that he has been saving

The original :

> 1856 - *You are the 1st to find this box - all the treasure has been moved - Here is the code*
>
> [encoded ciphertext]

1856 - You are the 1st to find this box – all the treasure has been moved – Here is the code you are the only one who knows about this. There were too many people trying to look for this. We loaded up our 4 ships and moved the treasure to the following four locations. Argos, Cádiz, Colchester, Cork. – ask for the shipbuilder he will safeguard this for you - you figure it out and its yours to keep.

Argos, Cádiz, Colchester, Cork – shipbuilders that have been in business around 1856.

"So what next…? Mrs Singh asks

""well these sound like ancient cities or towns.. we need to find out where they were and then look for ancient shipbuilders without involving anyone else…" was Mr Singh's reply.

"Ok… let me see… Argos, Cádiz, Colchester, Cork…."

The kids are tucked in for the night and these two get to work… Mr Singh pulls out another piece of paper and shws her - **Argos** (Greece) ; **Cadiz** (Spain); **Colchester** (Great Britain); **Cork** (Ireland) …

"Looks like our family is going to go on a trip to Europe… " Says Mr Singh… "But where is Mr Khanna and his team ??" Mrs Singh asks…

"South America – I found four cities in South America and our friends are there looking for the treasure… far away from europe…."

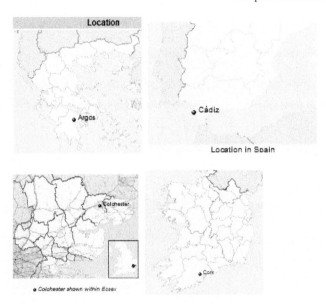

This is the game plan....

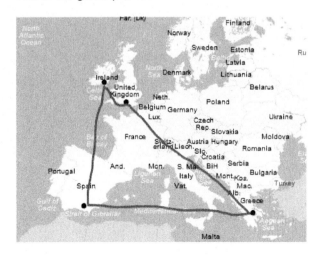

"Let us make a list of problems we could face... and make sure we have covered all our bases when we go out there...." Mrs Singh says this pulling out her laptop.

What do we do with the kids ?
Should we take our time and tackle one site at a time ? see if we can get the treasure... cause for all you know the treasure could be lost or taken away in the past 150 years...
If we find it what do we do with it ? Cause taking it across borders could be a problem...
How do we handle the locals and the trouble makers ?

Mrs Singh proposes:
Kids ... we take with us cause we don't want them left here by themselves
We do one site at a time.... Cause we don't know what we are getting into and lets take it slow...
I will contact some "rich treasure hunters" that I came across in my line of work and see if I can work out a deal with them.

Locals we are just going to have to play it by ear and if there is a slight hint of any problem we leave…

What do you think… she asks her husband….

"I agree to all your points except the 1st one… Kids don't go with us and neither do you .. you stay here… I need someone on the outside to help and let me just go there as a tourist and test the waters and see what I can find…. I will start with Argos, Greece"… he replies…

"Ok.. sounds good…

I will arrange for a diplomatic passport from you from Canada

I will get you an international non traceable phone…

I will use disposable calling cards and call you 9pm local time everyday…

If you don't answer the third call I will call the local consulate and they will help you…

If you feel the slight bit threatened just call this number 998989899 which would be strictly for your call…

Don't get too flashy out there just act normal... I will have collectors waiting in the wings to pickup and store the findings if any... if not just visit Greece and come back..."

"Ok sounds good... " Mr Singh agrees and hugs her.... And the journey begins....

Mr Singh and his wife were sipping coffee the night before he left. He walked into his study and opened a 1856 bible out of which he pulled out 4 pieces of clothing... and one picture. Walked out to his wife and said," I need to show you something...". and he handed them to her saying...,"This is also what I found in the tunnel but was afraid to show it to anyone. I have a feeling that these are the keys to the treasure... But I am not sure how these would be linked to the treasure... so don't whisper a word to anyone I will take a copy of these with me when I travel and keep the originals in a safe box."

His wife looked stunned; she was scared but knew that Mr Singh had a reason not to tell her this.

He took his hold book with him cut a small slice through the leather cover and slid the items in there. Before he did that he had a copy of each one of them with him.

The 1st leg....

He called his friend DON in Greece said that he is doing some research on ancient cities in Europe and ARGOS – in Greece is one of them. He just told him that he needs this research for his Phd. Don loved this idea and called up Peter in Argos who had a furniture business. So Mr Singh flew to Athens and drove down to Argos. Met him at the central library looking for books on ancient Greece and history of ARGOS. Peter met Mr. Singh and asked him if he wanted to go get some lunch. At lunch peter started talking about his family and business – his furniture business that they have been in for over 200 years. Mr Singh didn't know how to tell Peter what he was there for but hoping that if peter is in the furniture business which basically is still hand made in ARGOS he should know some of the old carpenter families in the area so he kept listening and nodding his head. Peter helped him checkout some books out of the library that were about 100 years old on businesses in ARGOS. Before he left he asked Mr Singh to come over to his house for dinner. Mr. Singh agreed ... took all the books to his hotel room and started reading.

Argos (Greek: Ἄργος, Árgos, [ˈarɣos]) is a city and a former municipality in Argolis, Peloponnese, Greece. It is 11 kilometres from Nafplion, which was its historic harbour. A settlement of great antiquity, Argos has been continuously inhabited for the past 7,000 years, making it one of the oldest cities in Greece and Europe. At the beginning of the Greek War of Independence in 1821, when many petty local republics were formed in different parts of the country, the "Consulate of Argos" was proclaimed on 26 May 1821, under the Senate of the Peloponnese.

Notable people

Acrisius, mythological king

Acusilaus (6th century BC), logographer and mythographer

Ageladas (6th-5th century BC), sculptor

Pheidon (7th century BC), king of Argos

Polykleitos (5th-4th century BC), sculptor

Polykleitos the Younger (4th century BC), sculptor

Telesilla (6th century BC), Greek poet

Eleni Bakopanos (1954-), Canadian politician

Argos was a powerful rival of Sparta for dominance over the Peloponnese, but was eventually shunned by other Greek city-states after remaining neutral during the Greco-Persian Wars. Numerous ancient monuments can be found in the city today, the most famous of which is the renowned Heraion of Argos, though agriculture (particularly citrus production) is the mainstay of the local economy.

Mr Singh found this old ancient place.. he naturally loved old ruins and thought of going there before he went to Peters house for dinner. He walked around the ruins for a while and wondered that the land that he was walking on was inhabited for over 7,000 years…WOW !!! is the only thing that came to his mind… he took some pictures with his digital camera and took a break on one of the fallen pillars. He keeps looking at the old ruins and noticed some numbers on a pillar 37.634642N 22.726580E – He wrote this down in his diary and didn't know what it ment. Well didn't worry about it much put it in his pocket and called Peter to confirm his dinner time…

It was 7:30PM he took a cab to Peters house. He was greeted by Peter his brother SAM and his parents. They talked about their family and their business and the ancient greek … Mr Singh Talked about India and the Indus valley and he fact that Alexander the great was in India around

326BC which apparently was his last stop conquering the world and turned back... so technically he did not rule India. They all laughed and Mr Singh pulls out his diary to write down his brother's (historian) number.

As soon as he opened his diary he noticed the numbers he had noted down when he visited the ruins... He showed that to his brother and told him where he got it from. Well SAM looked at the numbers and pulled out his laptop. He fed the numbers in his software and after churning the numbers it popped out the answer...

Looking at that shocked Mr Singh – SAM and Peter – it was the location of the current "Archaeological Museum of Argos"

"The history of the museum began in 1932, when the heirs of J. Kallergis donated the building to the Argos city council. They in turn gave it to the Greek state along with the surrounding area in 1955." Sam the historian explained. "But why was that on the pillar and for how long was it there??? And how come Mr Singh stumbled on it". He invited Mr. Singh to his office. Mr Singh's head was spinning. He had no idea what was going to happen and what he was getting involved in but agreed to meet SAM in his office. Next morning at 10 am Mr Singh is there with his diary – they had coffee and Sam suggested that they go to the museum and check it out .... They walk around and were checking the exhibits. Mr Singh looks at it and takes a picture just like he did others... He spend the rest of the morning taking pictures after pictures and then went to the nearest coffee shop pulled out his laptop and loaded all the pics... He knew there was a sign ... he just couldn't see it....

He had taken pictures of vases and paintings...buildings and ruins... He started listing down the collections to see how these would make sense and where it would lead to

The collections include :

Findings from Argos and the surounding area dated back from the Middlehellenic period(about 2000 B.C.) until the Postroman times(600 B.C.).

Findings of the American School of Classical Studies from Lerna(Myloi) dated between the Neolithic and Mycenaen times(5000 - 1100 B.C.).

Findings of the French Archaelogical School from the ancient Market, the area of the theatre - ancient and Roman - and the Mycenaen grave in Deras.

He also compiled the pictures and set up a slide show to see if he could find something... he kept narrowing the pics for detailed study and then thought it would lead him to something.

He had his diary with him, Sam was gone and he just kept sipping on coffe trying to figure things out...

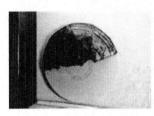

He had these pictures in a slideshow on his laptop trying to figure out suddenly he realized that the picture NO:3 looked very familiar. He reached out for his diary and pulled out the copy of the articles... as soon as he saw them... he fell off the chair...

Here is why....

Four out of the five items he had in his possession was in the picture... He could not believe what he was seeing... He was sitting there all by himself cause SAM had to meet with a client. Now things were getting complicated and simpler at the same time... He was looking at a puzzle and trying to put it together. He knew that all these ment something together but never knew what to do next and had 100's of questions running through his mind – some of the things that were running through his mind were...

What were all of his pictures doing together in that picture?

Link to the Treasure...

How are these linked to the treasure?

What is the picture of the man doing there?

This I believe has taken a new turn.....

Ok.. He rushes back to the library and calls SAM ... puts everything on the table and arranges it in a manner similar to the picture...

SAM gets there... Mr Singh... asks him," What do all these set in this order tell you ?"

"These are the **Secret Symbols of the Rosicrucians**, The Rosicrucian order is generally believed to have been the idea of a group of German protestants in the 1600s when a series of three documents were published: Fama Fraternitatis Rosae Crucis, Confessio Fraternitatis, and The Chymical Wedding of Christian Rosenkreutz anno 1459. The documents were so widely read and influential, that the historian Frances Yeats refers to the 17th century as the Rosicrucian Enlightenment. The first document tells the story of a mysteriousalchemist (Christian Rosenkreuz) who travelled to various parts of the world gathering secret knowledge. The second document tells of a secret brotherhood of alchemists who were preparing to change the political and intellectual face of Europe. The third document describes the invitation of Christian Rosenkreuz to attend and assist at the "Chemical" wedding of a King and Queen in a castle of Miracles.

Current members of the Rosicrucian Order claim that its origins are far more ancient than these documents. The authors of the documents seemed to strongly favor Lutheranism and include condemnations of the Catholic Church. Rosicrucianism probably had an influence on Masonry and, in fact, the 18th degree of Scottish Rite Masonry is called the Knight of the Rose Croix (red cross).

There are a large number of Rosicrucian groups today – each claiming to be closely tied to the original. Of the two main divisions, one is a mix of

Christianity with Rosicrucian principles, and the other is semi-Masonic. The Masonic type tend to also have degrees of membership. The last man who was leading this was Sir William Paterson...."

"So its William Peterson who would be the link between the clues, the treasure – but who is this guy and who are these Rosicrucians" Mr Singh was just confused.. but he knew he was headed in the right direction...

"I think you might want to talk to my dad he would be able to shed more light on the **Rosicrucians",** SAM suggested.

There was this place in the park across the museum where his dad played chess every evening and mingled with his friends. Mr Singh thought that would be the best place to meet him... Later that day he put the four clues in his pocket with his digital camera and went over to the park. They were all playing chess there was a board empty, Mr Singh sat there and started setting up the board. SAM's father Joseph walks up to him..."Aaa- HA- I get to play chess with an Indian – who invented this game...- wow"... they both sat... started talking about their pasts and travels. Mr Singh mentioned that he is doing research on Lost cities – oldest cities in the world and ARGOS was one of them... He then pulled out the 4 clues and set it on the table..."Do you know anything about this ?" SAM asked....

This instantly wiped the smile off of Joseph's face. "What happened ?"... He asked... "I don't want to talk about it ". Joseph replied...

"You don't want to talk about it – Why ??".. Mr Singh asked.

 "Lets just say that its personal and I rather not discuss this.... "

"NNONONONO You have to tell me... come on ... don't do this".. Mr Singh insisted.

"Well if you beat me in a game of chess.. I might think about it..." Joseph offered.

Mr Singh a gambler himself replied with a counter offer," if I beat you in less than 6 moves you will not just tell me about this but also your involvement in this – agreed????" Saying that he extended his hand ...

Seeing that three of Josephs friends walked up to the table.... Joseph whispered in one of the guys ear and they whispered to each other in greek. Mr Singh just realized that there is more to it and that If he gets these guys to help it would work out best...

Going back in time....

"DEAL !!!" Joseph shook Mr Singh's hand and they both sat... "If you beat me in more than 6 steps you never bring this up for as long as you live..."

They were surrounded by three of his friends – Mr Singh made the 1st move, Joseph followed, Singh repeated, joseph countered... in his 5th move Mr Singh declared a check mate and defeated Joseph. Joseph couldn't believe it... but a deal was a deal... so Joseph asked Mr Singh to meet him at the ruins next to the third pillar standing at 6 AM tomorrow morning.

Mr Singh shook his hand and left. Needless to say he could not sleep all night. Religiously his wife called and he narrated all to her ... she was shocked and knew that her husband was not in any danger but asked him to take care of himself. 5AM Mr Singh was ready and decided to walk to the ruins a km from where he lived. He wore his traditional Pajama Kurta embroidered that looked very traditional and entered the ruins... he walked around... saw a dog sitting there and an eagle on one of the standing pillars. There were only four pillars standing... One had a vulture on it one had an eagle on it one with a raven on it but on the third pillar there was nothing. He walked to the pillar and stood there... As the clock stuck 6 he saw four men walking towards him in black robes. The hoods covered their faces as they got closer Mr Singh stood straight. They stood around him and in one tone said "THIS IS THE GOLDEN AND ROSY CROSS, MADE OF PURE GOLD, WHICH EVERY BROTHER WEARS ON HIS BREAST." As they said that Joseph pulled out a creed and rolled it out... he pinned it to the pillar and they all raised their right hand over their head as to salute ..

as the robe slid over the arm he saw  tattooed on their arm. We are all brothers have been for hundreds of years have protected the faith and shall do for the next 1000 years. We have been a secret society for over 450 years. Our brothers have supported us by taking from the rich and helping the needy as our faith believed in for centuries. Joseph pulled out a small silk pouch and gave it to Mr Singh and said,"We have been waiting for you for over 200 years this belongs to you".

Mr Singh takes it uts it in his coat pocket the four turn around and walk away in the four directions. He looks at the pillars and so does tha raven, vulture and eagle fly away... He dare not open the silk pouch there so he walks back to his room and sets it on the table, before he could open it he walked up to the window to close the curtain – he sees two huge men outside wearing black robes like the priest would wear standing in guard as guarding the place. Well there is nothing he could do so he walks back to his desk opens the pouch and pulls out a tin box out 3" X 2" which was sealed with wax and had a SEAL stamped on the top. He pulls out his knife and opens it up.... He couldnot believe his eyes.... It had a picture in it of Sir William Paterson. The same picture he had in his possession at the back of this picture it said... "founder of the Bank of England – Our guardian"

He knew for sure that Joseph had no idea what was in the box so he decided to go dig deeper in doing research on Mr Paterson. The next evening he walks up to the park sees the men there and just nods his head as saying "Thanks"... does not talk but plays a few games of chess and has a cup of coffee. As they were getting ready to leave he walks over to Joseph and asks him,"What do you know about Mr William Paterson ? "
"Just what everyone else knows..." Joseph replies...
"What do you mean ????" Mr Singh asks...
Pointing at the central library he says,"second floor – L5 – you will see..." and they walk away...
Mr Singh wasted no time.. ran towards the library.... goes up to stairs but there is a sign that says "RESTRICTED" he walks up to the the front desk and asks... there is this 21 year old sitting there checking out books looks

over to him and says,"There are manuscripts up there not touched for 100s of years,... no one is allowed ther". Mr Singh looks at his watch its 8:45PM in 15 mins the library closes... He walks around – there is an announcement that the library is to close in 15 min please checkout your books. He walks around and notices a few things...

3 exits – 1 chained – rest two have keypad access. No guards anywhere except the front door. Second floor has a keypad code access. He finally finds a place to hid – there was a location where two book shelves met at 90degree and there was a space behind it.

Library closes at 9:00 by 9:30 the people leave and Mr Singh is left alone.at 9:45 he walks up to the second floor and is standing in front of the keypad and starts entering different combinations to get in... kept trying for over an hour absolutely frustrated.... He starts looking through his diary and starts looking for clues... he reads.. "Consulate of Argos" was proclaimed on 26 May 1821.

He enters 2612 an BINGO it opens... how did he get that ... well 26 from the date and 12 = 1+8+2+1.

He walks up to L5 and starts looking at books – picks up one that said "Politics"

Bank of England Connection...

He sits on the bench and starts looking at the pages.. he finally finds this picture – and is shocked with what is written underneath...

Sir William Paterson (pictured), founder of the Bank of England, is suspected to have been a pirate in his years before founding the bank.

Good lord.... Now it all makes sense....

Rosicrucians : Secret society

Linked to the pirates and stolen loot from 1300 to about 1800 for 500 years.

They hid the loot in different islands

In 1694, he founded the Bank of England

He help fund different British ventures through this bank

With little or no compliances and checks it was easy for him to clean the loot.

He has proof of the Rosicrucians and knows that William Peterson is linked to it and the four cities but now the million dollar question is how does he get to the loot.

As far as Joseph and all his acquaintances in ARGOS knew he was just doing research for his Phd.

Gets Mr Singh thinking – well I am going to have to track William Petersons movements – this charter will give him access to the societies and he will have to find the clues along the way…

While he was thinking and reading…he read a name of a co-Pirate **John Holland…** and a few pages later discovered that John Holland was a founder of the Bank of Scotland, in 1695.

This was too much to digest…Two of the greatest pirates of the 18th century finally cleaned up their loot via two of the greatest banks on the world and there were millions of dollars worth of loot still in hiding and that is what he will have to find. 1st leg of his visit is successful. He goes back to the back door with the code enters the same code and walks out – before he left he took digital pictures of the pages. He got out of the library and walked away to his room. Called his wife downloaded the docs and pics and info. Talked to her and explained what he had deduced. Mr. Singh finally slept and before he slept he looked at the list of places he had to visit **Argos** (Greece) ;

Cadiz (Spain);

Colchester (Great Britain);

Cork (Ireland)

With all the leads coming from the UK area he decided to go there next...

Watch out Brits…

Mr Singh calls his cousin Rocky in Birmingham he had not seen in almost 10 years. Who was happy to hear from him and was happy that Mr Singh was coming over to meet him. Rocky was an antiques dealer in England and had been for almost 20 years. Very well known in his line of work and very well respected. Mr Singh arrived and Rocky took him strait to his shop – Rocky wanted to show him some old antiques that he had just pickup at a local church auction. Mr Singh looked his collections some old paintings and books and some WWII medals. Just the general stuff. While Rocky was busy going through his accounts Mr. Singh asks him ,"Hey Rocky have you heard of **Colchester ?"**

Rocky stops writing looks up at Mr Singh and said," did you say Colchester ??? the ancient city Colchester?"

Mr Singh nods his head. "Where did you ever come across that city?, did you know that Colchester is known as the oldest recorded Roman town in Britain, Colchester claims to be the oldest town in Britain. It was for a time the capital of Roman Britain and also claims to have the United Kingdom's oldest recorded market." Rocky explained.

Mr Singh explains,"well I am working on my Phd and one of the sections of my research is ancient cities and Colchester is one of them..".

"Well here is another interesting fact about your city - Colchester is reputed to be the home of three of the best known English nursery rhymes: 'Old King Cole', 'Humpty Dumpty' and 'Twinkle, Twinkle Little Star'... and I am not making this up..." Rocky replied smiling... Well let me know what you need for your research and I Can dig up come old books for you to read...

Mr Singh was surprised.. thanked Rocky and walked towards the stairs to go to the second floor of Rocky's collection. With all the information he had he just didn't know how he is going to get to the treasure... oh well he thought you never know.... He looks around and finds some neat artifacts some cheap some expensive...he collects a few old books from the late 1800's about history of Essex county. On his way out Rocky asked him, "hey I am headed that way to pick up some stuff from a senior do you want to join me ?"

Mr Singh agreed... after a long drive Rocky stopped by "The Brick Layers Pub" looked like a family run pub in Colchester....

"Is this where you are going to meet him ?" Singh asked.

"Yup this is where he spends his evenings and has been doing that for almost 70 years"

"70 years ??? how old is this guy ? 100...?" Singh inquired...

"Well almost – he is 95 years old a walking encyclopedia... you wanna meet him or not?"

Mr Singh shrug his shoulder .. I have no choice.. ok....

They walked in and in the corner there was sitting an old man sipping on his drink with a bag.

"Hi, this is my friend Mr Singh ... doing his Phd and was doing some research on old cities.. and I know you are th oldest man alive in the oldest town in England..." Rocky introduced Andrew...

"Mr Singh, this is Andrew Smith his family has lived here since 1189, when Colchester was granted its first royal charter by King Richard I – so no book in give you the information that Andrew and his family can.

Andrew pulls out a few old books from mid 1700's some paintings on cloth rolled them out on the table and looked at Rocky ... as if asking him to look at the stuff and make him an offer. Mr Singh picks up the painting and looks at it... in the corner of the painting he notices something... which was not too clear cause the lights were too low.. he pulls out his cell phone and turns on the built in flash light focuses on the painting and his heart skips a beat…. He looks at Andrew and asks him," I like this one would look cool on my wall … do you have any more?" Andrew pulls a few more out – all of them 18" X 11" size … Mr Singh picks five out of them and separates them.. he asks Andrew what he wanted for them.

"Make me an offer I can't refuse…" Andrew replied…

"How about $150 each $750 for all five ?" Mr Singh replies…

Rocky looks at Mr Singh,"are you nuts I wouldn't pay more that $50 for each… its your money.. watch it"…

Rocky walks towards the restroom … Andrew looks at Mr Singh "Ok – you got a deal"… Mr Singh pulls out dollars – cause that is all he had and paid Andrew…. "Can I ask why you picked these five from the 12 I had on the table " he asked…

"Well I just liked them .. that's all and they would match my walls..", replied Mr. Singh…

"What secret society are you a member off ?" Andrew asked…

"WHAT ?", Mr. Singh acted surprised..

"For every painting you focused on the bottom left corner... you only picked the ones that had the "signs/codes" that are linked to secret society... and I am almost 100 years old... if you are looking for something I might be able to help you.. Remember I am the oldest person in the oldest town in England..." Andrew explained...

He pulled a napkin and drew these signs

Mr Singh just looked at him and signaled him to keep mum. He could see Rocky coming back...

Rocky just got back... he looked at the other stuff made an offer on a few items and paid Andrew.. just before leaving he looked at Mr Singh and said,"why don't you come back tomorrow and I will show you the town...".

Mr Singh shook his hand and thanked him... Rocky and Mr Singh left long drive back Rocky kept talking about how he started his business on how he started and how he grew...   His best find was a charter of one of the dukes in Scotland that he picked up at an auction for £25 – which was later picked up by a Japanese collector for £10,000.

He went on and on and on… and Mr Singh just played along until Rocky mentions old MAPS… Rocky had picked up a whole box of old maps for £100 that was anywhere from 100-500 years old…

"Did you say old maps???"… Singh asked…

"Yes you wanna see them ? I have them at home … you can look at them, will cut you a great deal..", he said winking at Mr Singh.

Mr Singh couldn't wait to get home and rushed to the basement where Rocky had the maps… they opened up the box and rolled each map.. there were about 25 of them. Mr Singh kept looking at them trying to find something that might have been of any interest for him. He just couldn't find anything of interest … 2 cups of coffee two hours later… he looked lost. Rocky was watching TV he looked at Mr Singh and said,"If you want to go and meet Andrew again I can arrange for a place for you to live there to peacefully do your research… let me know"

Mr Singh wanted to meet with Andrew and pick his brain, "sure … I would love to stay in his town and just study its history… sure" he replied.

He wanted to do that anyways – now he will have a chance at staying there he can concentrate on his research and finding the "treasure"… This was turning out to be a bit complicated but there was always hope…

Mrs Singh used to call religiously every night to make sure all is well with her husband and was taking down notes, she would record their conversations and then type them out… she would mark every tape write down the date, time and location – she kept a good record of everything…

Research in Rome getting deep...

During the talk his wife mentioned that he might be getting into some dangerous territory and asked him to be carefull... The next day armed with all of his information Mr. Singh check into **The George Hotel : is classified as historic**

This 500 year old coaching inn sits in the oldest town in England, Colchester. The extensive medieval cellars, preserved behind glass, detail soil from old Roman roads and even the ashes left by the fires of Queen Boudicca's rampage in AD60

He checks in and calls his wife and gives her all the information. He then calls Andrew and lets him know that he is there. Andrew is thrilled... and they decide that they will meet for dinner... after the call Mr Singh pulls out his

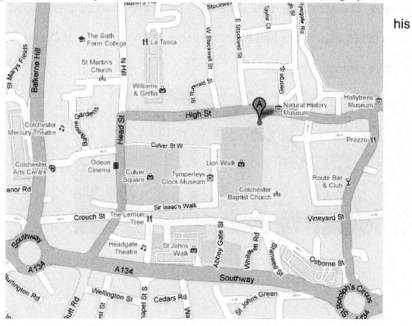

laptop and gets the map around the hotel

100 meters from Tymperleys Clock Museum

200 meters from Colchester Castle Museum

300 meters from Colchester Natural History Museum

400 meters from Hollytrees Museum

Colchester Castle Museum is what he is interested in just visit... He calls Andrew back and asks if he can get access to the museum. Andrew said he cannot get access to the museum because its too late however he knows a few folks that can get him access to the castle – excluding the museum. Mr Singh is thrilled... great !!!

Mr Andrew shows up at the hotel in his buggy – he sits with Mr Singh and they start talking about history. Andrew tells him how his family laid the stone for this hotel building in 1490. He was interested in knowing why Mr Singh picked those paintings and if he had any connection with the secret society. As the conversation took a turn in that direction Mr Singh knew that he had a mistake once with Mr Khanna and wanted to keep the treasure story a secret. He explained to

Andrew that his research was also connected to various secret societies and ancient cities and the sign that he saw on those paintings was a clue that they are linked. He mentioned the Rosicrucians : Secret society. This is what he is concentrating on… he ordered a drink for Andrew and just wanted to listen to what he had to say. "Now that is a society you need to be a part of... most of the rich and famous men in this country were directly or indirectly related to this society... and there are rumors that there is a chosen family from the east that is a rightful owner of treasures that are still hidden... there are codes that they need to decipher to get to the treasure. No one knows what form this treasure is 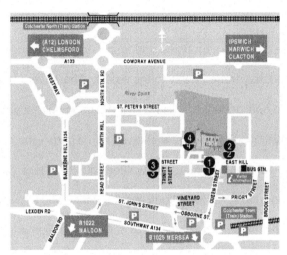 in but it has been sitting somewhere for over 500 years. Another interesting thing is that the castle is where the members met... this is where they had been meeting for over 500 years... For most of its life the Castle was used as a prison. One of the most infamous episodes in its history occurred in 1645 when Matthew Hopkins, the self-styled Witchfinder General, used the Castle to imprison and interrogate suspected witches. The Castle first opened to the public as a museum in 1860." Andrew rattled off the complete history of the society and castle and pulls out a picture of the castle that he had brought with him.

"Wow that is some history.. well lets go to the castle and see what we can find tonight.

They ordered dinner and discussed more of the history of the city... Once done they walked outside and found Andrew's buggy – Mr. Singh hopped in and they trotted away to the castle. There were torches lit and a guard stood outside as soon as he saw the buggy he stepped forward asking for identification. Mr Andrew showed him a card – the gates were opened and they were let in. The guard walked with them took care of the buggy and called a "keeper" to walk us into the castle and show us its history. Colchester was the first capital of Roman Britain and beneath the Castle are the remains of the most famous Roman buildings, the Temple of Claudius. Today if you lay your hand on the stonework of the temple it can be said that you are touching the very foundation of Roman Britain.
He walked them to different sections and showed them the 2000 year history of the place. The castle was used as a prison for many years and they walked into the place where the prison guards and soldiers would sit and relax ... the benches were made of stone the walls were stone, the entrance to the room was not a normal door it was a metal door like a prison door with a huge latch... They walk in and sit on the bench...

Andrew excuses himself and walks out of the room to used the bathroom. Meanwhile the "keeper" follows him ... while Mr Singh is admiring the walls and paintings he hears "CLANG..." The door is shut and locked. He turns around there is no one not even the keeper. He calls out to Mr Andrew – no answer... at first he thinks it's a joke he waits for a while after about 30 mins reality sinks in – this was a trap. He pulls out his phone and no signal. All he can see is stone walls and an iron door... Without panicking he sits and starts thinking ...

He knows that every place like this has more than one entry... now how should he find it.. he walks up to the lit up torch and walks around the room surveying it to see if he can find a clue. He walks over to every painting on the wall – they are all nailed to the wall. He tries to push them move them to find the trap door – but nothing.. Nothing at all... frustrated and two hours later he thinks he should just lie down on the bench for the night and in the morning when the castle folks show up he can get out.

He lies down and in a few mins the torch is off except for the oil lamp in the corner there is nothing. He falls asleep .. around 3 AM he feels heat on his hand and opens his eye ... he sees 5 men wearing a black cloak hoods and lit torches in each hand. Their cloaks had these embroidered on it. He knew that these folks are not there to get him out but to find out what he was doing there and that they knew that he had information about their society. He woke up rubbing his eyes. He was surrounded by the five men and the one in the center looked at him and said.........

The final countdown... A shocker...

"WELCOME !!! we have been waiting for you ...you have come a lot further than anyone in 200 years. You will stay here no harm to you – however we need for you to get the untouched "treasure" to its rightful owner. Let me be very clear Mr Singh – Either you help us and find the right full owner or you never see the light of day again – ", the one in the center explains...

Mr Singh is confused .." How am I going to help you find the right full owner ?"

"We were told that the man who gets this far will know who the right full owner is and where the treasures have been sitting for the past 200 years. So rest in this room next door – you will be provided with all your basic needs and guarded. You will get clues and you have to decipher them – that will help us unlock the code and find the chosen one." Saying this he was lead to the room next door with a bed, table and a chair. And they all left.

Meanwhile Mrs Singh has been frantically calling no reply no answer... She had alerted the London undercover police who were at the "The George

Hotel" and looking for Andrew. They tracked him down in his house and take him to the nearest interrogation center. He kept on saying that he has never met Mr Singh. The police had no proof and all they could do was intimidate this almost 100 year old man. They locked him in a room and left to discuss what needs to be done next. After discussing all the odds they thought they would go to the hotel and see if they can find any more clues but would take Andrew with them. They walk into the room to get him and find that there was no one... except a note on the table saying "*Here is wisdom. Let him that hath understanding count the number of the beast: for it is the number of a man; and his number is ?*"

What was that ? they all wondered – 666 is what they thought but what was that note doing there and how would that lead it to Mr Singh. John Masterson took a picture of the note and emailed it to Mrs Singh – Mrs Singh with an IQ of 140 – worried about her husband had deciphered tons of codes in her life and was well known for that. She takes that and starts working on it... she knew that the note "*Here is wisdom. Let him that hath understanding count the number of the beast: for it is the number of a man; and his number is....*" Is not as simple as 666.

Mummy goes to the land of mummies...

She goes through the note and starts her research. Well versed in Latin and greek she pulls out some old manuscripts. Starts looking and all of a sudden she picks up the phone and sends her friend Alexis in Egypt a message " I am coming to Egypt with my kids" She goes to her kids and tells them that they are going to see the pyramids. The kids are thrilled... they are happy and start packing... they love in – 24 hours later they are in Cairo. Alexis picks them up and arranges for their stay. She lays out a plan for the sightseeing that the kids are going to go ... Mrs Singh starts on a trip... they go from place to place.. kids are having a great time... They were having lunch close to the pyramids when Mrs Singh looks at Alexis and asks her," how far is Oxyrhynchus ? why don't we go there next?"

"Oxyrhynchus ? that place .. no one really goes there... why do you want to go there... she asks...

"For the past century, the area around Oxyrhynchus has been continually excavated, yielding an enormous collection of papyrus texts dating from the time of the Ptolemaic and Roman periods of Egyptian history. Among the texts discovered at Oxyrhynchus are plays of Menander and fragments of the Gospel of Thomas, an early Christian document. I want to visit some old antique dealers there...", Mrs Singh replies.

"Oxyrhynchus is a city in Upper Egypt, located about 160 km south-southwest of Cairo, in the governorate of Al Minya, sure we can go there tomorrow" – Alexis assures.

"I hope my husband is fine... and I hope I can decipher this code..." Mrs Singh keeps worrying.

Later that evening she goes through her maps to see where the city is at –

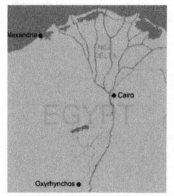

She knows that there are places where she can find some old texts and try to decipher the code...

She picks up an book on ancient history. And reads more about Oxyrhynchos. ," For more than 1,000 years, the inhabitants of Oxyrhynchus dumped garbage at a series of sites out in the desert sands beyond the town limits. The fact that the town was built on a canal rather than on the Nile itself was important, because this meant that the area did not flood every year with the rising of the river, as did the districts along the riverbank. When the canals dried up, the water table fell and never rose again. The area west of the Nile has virtually no rain, so the garbage dumps of Oxyrhynchus were gradually covered with sand and were forgotten for another 1,000 years.

Because Egyptian society under the Greeks and Romans was governed bureaucratically, and because Oxyrhynchus was the capital of the 19th nome, the material at the Oxyrhynchus dumps included vast amounts of paper. Accounts, tax returns, census material, invoices, receipts, correspondence on administrative, military, religious, economic, and political matters, certificates and licenses of all kinds—all these were periodically cleaned out of government offices, put in wicker baskets, and dumped out in the desert. Private citizens added their own piles of unwanted paper. Because papyrus was expensive, paper was often reused: a document might have farm accounts on one side, and a student's text of Homer on the other. TheOxyrhynchus Papyri, therefore, contained a complete record of the life of the town, and of

the civilizations and empires of which the town was a part. ' This brings hope... she knows that the code of the beast she can definitely find here... They get there and she asks Alexis to take her around to the places where this place was used as a dumping ground. They get there in a jeep... kids are having fun... enjoying....she surveys the market place and finally discovers that "Barkat Ali" was the most prestigious antique dealer in manuscripts and the most reputed one. His family had been historians and has a mass collection of manuscripts. This man would charge a fee just to enter his shop. He would charge money by the hour to just browse through the manuscripts – he would not sell any manuscripts to a person only to museums. Mrs Singh asks Alexis to go take the kids out to old shops and shop for things while she looks at old manuscript. She walks into the shop showing here candian ID. She asks for manuscripts from the turn of the century – when Jesus Christ was crucified. He takes her to a room that was guarded with heavy security code. He pulls out these huge leather bound books and places them on a table... "There you go lady.. remember you are charged by the hour on the credit card you presented and if it wasn't for the secret service ID we would have not even entertained you.. so have fun and when done pick up that phone and call us we will come get you – meanwhile Ali Hassan will be here to help you and make sure you don't damage any of the manuscripts." He instructs her and leaves.

She starts looking at the manuscripts and lays them out on the table. She arranges them in order making sure they are all set in the right time line.

She opens a page and while reading the manuscript she kept playing with her locket. Hassan ali was sitting not too far looking at what she was reading and when done an hour later she asks to speak to Barkat Ali. He dials the no and is instructed to come down. She asks him if she can buy a few pages... He refuses. She offers twice as what the museum would offer. He refuses – apologizes.. she is lead out of the place and charge $500 on her card for the hour and a half reading the docs and the entrance fee.

Mrs Singh smiles and walks out. She hurriedly calls Alexis and asks her to return back home. She sits in the back seat and opens up her laptop – pulls out her locket and plugs it into the laptop – all the time at Barkat Ali's she had been taking HQ pics with a camera hidden in her locket. She downloaded about 150 pics into the laptop. The entire journey was over 3 hours and she couldn't wait to go home so she satarts looking at the

pictures. She knew a bit greek and Latin so anything that she thought was important she sorted out. When she had them sorted out she had about 10 documents that she had to translate.

Fourth century fragment from the Oxyrhynchus papyri, the ancient equivalent of paper.

Rev 13:18 Here is wisdom. Let him that hath understanding count the number of the beast: for it is χιϛ *the number of a man; and his number*

She was shocked when she saw that .... The Greeks wrote numbers with letters from their alphabet so the sequence χιϛ (Chi Iota Stigma) in the text fragment shown above represents the number 600 + 10 + 6 or 616.

α Alpha	1	ι Iota	10	ρ Rho	100
β Beta	2	κ Kappa	20	σ / ϛ Sigma	200
γ Gamma	3	λ Lamda	30	τ Tau	300
δ Delta	4	μ Mu	40	υ Upsilon	400
ε Epsilon	5	ν Nu	50	φ Phi	500
ϛ Stigma	6	ξ Xi	60	χ Chi	600
ζ Zeta	7	o Omicron	70	ψ Psi	700
η Eta	8	π Pi	80	ω Omega	800
θ Theta	9	G Koppa	90	ϡ Sampi	900

Anti Christ Connection 666 or 616

By the time they reached Cairo she was done with her research...
Here it is ...

there are apparently two different spellings of the word "beast" in Hebrew which also produce **the numbers 666 and 616.**
The standard form therefore according to Irenaeus was χξϚ (Chi Xi Stigma) or 600 + 60 + 6 = 666 and any other version is in error. The purpose of this number was to enable the faithful to recognise the Antichrist when he finally emerged and it was given in a numeric rather than literal form
because even the very name of the Antichrist was an abomination and as such not worthy of mention in the holy book. Irenaeus explains that the number is derived from a common Greek practice of calculating numbers from names known as Isopsephy (or Gematria in Hebrew*). The usual way was to convert the letters of the person's name into numbers and then simply add them together 616. For 2000 years, 666 has been the number of the dreaded anti-Christ. An unlucky number for many, even the European parliament leaves seat number 666 vacant. The number is from the book of Revelation, the last book of the Christian Bible.

She immediately calls her counterpart in Colchester and sends them the solution:

Rev 13:18 Here is wisdom. Let him that hath understanding count the number of the beast: for it is the number of a man; and his number 616...

Back in England...

June 12, 2011

As soon as the message was send the people were floored 616 –

Masterson the chief was wondering:

what is going on?

Where is Mr Singh ?

How is this connected to Mr Singh ?

How am I going to find Mr Singh... ?

He locks himself in the room that Andrew disappeared from....

Chief Masterson was very well respected in the law enforcement – he kept looking at the walls made of brick and stone.

He asked his men to leave him alone and only open the door when he calls...

He uses his stick and starts tapping on the walls thinking at the same time on where is Mr Andrew and where is Mr. Singh. While doing so he looks at the was a stool in the corner under a painting – he puts a foot on it and pushes it aside to get closer to the painting… "BAAAAAAAAAAAAAAAM" a trap door opens he falls down 15 feet. The door shuts and He is laying down on a stack of hay. Its dark but he sees a tunnel and strategically placed oil lamps.. he starts walking and following the lamps… after about 30 mins of walking he walks into a room which has a door at the opposite end with 9 blocks with numbers on the wall. He looks at the wall and then remembers 616 – He taps on the blocks in the same sequence 616 and braces himself. The wall rotates and Mr. Masterson sees Mr Singh sitting in front of him who was equally shocked – He looks at Mr Masterson and says," one more step and I will fight…"

Mr Masterson… explains the whole story – this is the tunnel through which Andrew escaped.. they looked back at the wall and the blocks were facing them. Mr Singh tried to push the wall .. Masterson asked him to step aside – punched 616 and the wall rotated.. they were out of the room. Without wasting any time they were out – they made sure that nothing was left behind – all was in order and they ran towards the trap door – end of the tunnel. Apparently the tunnel had many veins and this was spread across many houses in town off which very few knew except for the "chosen". The finally got to the point and didn't know how to open up the trap door... Masterson had Mr Singh stand on his shoulders and tried to open the door – never opened.. this was not what they were looking for and they knew that sooner or later they would find out that Mr Singh was missing and would be in the tunnel. They had to think fast they started to walk back and try one of the other veins they kept walking and reached the end of the vein another set of blocks with numbers... and what do you know the combnation is "616"... aaaha... the door / wall rotated and the stepped in .. looked like one of the storage rooms for a restaurant. They tiptoed into the room made sure the wall /door is closed and walked in – they had two doors in front of them. They looked at each other and couldn't decide... they look at the doors carefully. Mr Singh looks at the door on the left and says this one... from the bottom of the door there was a stream of light looked more like a safe bet... they pushed it and they were out on the street. They walked a few steps and couldn't believe they were a block away from "THE GEORGE HOTEL".

Masterson calls for backup and they escape from there. Mr Singh did not tell Masterson about the whole experience but called his wife and let her know he was safe. As their car was cruising and Masterson was talking to Mr Singh it was getting late and dark.. He asked the driver to steer towards "The Knights" for dinner… As soon as he said that the driver turned left and drove on. He drove for over 15 mins stopped at "The Knights" and had dinner. The left and Masterson asked the driver to drop him off at the station and drop Mr. Singh at "THE GEORGE HOTEL".

Mr Singh gets there acts as though nothing had happened gets into his room and relaxes.

The next morning he calls his wife and tells her that he needs to get away for a few days and not to worry. He assures her that all is well.

Mrs Singh called her husband and never got a reply except that she used to get a message from him every night "all is well". That is all he did.. what he did ? where he was ? who was with him ? what is going on ? no one knows…

Mrs Singh was worried kids kept asking about dad and tried to talk to him. There were times that he used to talk to his kids but its been a week and they hadn't been able to talk to dad.

One day Mrs Singh gets a call from The British Embassy – "Mrs Singh, is everything Ok ? Mr Singh is fine... you need not worry. If there is anything you need call us at this number".

She was surprised... didn't know what was going on... well at least she knew that Mr Singh was well.

Royalty at the doorstep...

A week later Mrs Singh was playing with the kids in the front yard and an official car marker "British Embassy" shows up at the gate. Mr Singh steps out a gentleman steps out and picks up Mr Singhs luggage. Walks to the door – Mr Singh tips him 1000 bucks...
Kids come and hug him Mr Singh hugs him glad to see the family back...
She asks the maid to make some tea and fritters for Mr Singh.
'After I got out of the castle I met with Andrew again and stayed with him for a week. He pulled out the history of the ships and loot – William Peterson had funded the bank from all of the pirate loot this loot was masked with the bank and that is how he avoided persecution. He used to collect loot from the ships find the rightful owners and his job was to guard this loot and pass it along to their family. Every loot had signs and codes that needed deciphered who so-ever deciphered the code and got to the "hidden society" they would be the rightful owners of the loot and just to make sure that the owners don't have to carry gold and silver and precious metal they were converted to pounds and deposited in the bank.

When the rightful owner showed up they "secret" society would verify and would hand over the account to them –in todays world the accounts are safe guarded by biometrics and are issued new code to make sure two owners don't show up and that chapter is closed." Mr Singh explained…

" So what are you telling me ??? that the island loot was hidden in the bank account and after all that you went through and toed the lose ends up you were actually the rightful owner of the loot ?... asked Mrs Singh…

"You and we get a royalty status"… Mr Singh replies… He pulls out his wallet and pulls out a card from it – shows it to his wife – "Royal Bank of England – Royal Account NO "FWIN66818245701-RA". Caretaker David Spence 1716. Who got a payment of Twelve pounds a month to take care of the royal account until handed over to the rightful owner… David Spencers family was paid over £ 50,000 plus interest for the past 300 years which amounts to close to £ 500,000 which was paid in lump sum to Phillip Spence who was present at my handover meeting in LONDON. "

"WOW !!! " is all Mrs Singh could say... and if you don't mind me asking after paying the caretakers how much do you still have in the account ?"
"Enough for our 6 generations... I would say " replies Mr Singh. Mr Singh opens up his hand carry bag and hands a remote control car to his son, He pulls out a beautiful dress for Simi and a diamond set for his wife. All of the items had a tag of "Harrods" on it.   Mrs Singh looks at her husband "HARRODS... ????"
"Yes dear Harrods... and I got to meet Prince Andrew and his bride Sophie. Before I left England". Mr Singh explained...

Mrs Singh was happy that the her husband was fine and all was well.. as they were discussing this their daughter comes in with a bunch of papers in her hand. " Papa here is a letter looks like its from a travel agency for a trip to CHINA.. what do you want me to do papa ?" she asks her papa

Mrs Singh looks at her daughter and smiles, "Tear it – rip it... ". I think we need a break from trips..." She gives her husband a hug and he smiles... "CHINA dear...?"

She puts her hand on his mouth and says.. don't you dare MR ROYALTY......

And the family lives happily ever after.. did they go to China ?????????? that's for you to find out,...

CPSIA information can be obtained
at www.ICGtesting.com
Printed in the USA
BVOW06s1959231217
503558BV00017B/797/P